Swedish Food & Cooking

Traditions · Ingredients · Tastes · Techniques · Over 60 Classic Recipes

Swedish Food & Cooking

Anna Mosesson

with photographs by William Lingwood

This edition is published by Aquamarine, an imprint of Anness Publishing Ltd Hermes House, 88–89 Blackfriars Road, London SE1 8HA tel. 020 7401 2077; fax 020 7633 9499 www.aquamarinebooks.com; www.annesspublishing.com

If you like the images in this book and would like to investigate using them for publishing, promotions or advertising, visit our website www.practicalpictures.com for more information.

© Anness Publishing Ltd 2006, 2007

UK agent: The Manning Partnership Ltd, 6 The Old Dairy, Melcombe Road, Bath BA2 3LR; tel. 01225 478444; fax 01225 478440; sales@manning-partnership.co.uk

UK distributor: Grantham Book Services Ltd, Isaac Newton Way, Alma Park Industrial Estate, Grantham, Lincs NG31 9SD; tel. 01476 541080; fax 01476 541061; orders@gbs.tbs-ltd.co.uk

North American agent/distributor: National Book Network, 4501 Forbes Boulevard, Suite 200, Lanham, MD 20706; tel. 301 459 3366; fax 301 429 5746; www.nbnbooks.com

Australian agent/distributor: Pan Macmillan Australia, Level 18, St Martins Tower, 31 Market St, Sydney, NSW 2000; tel. 1300 135 113; fax 1300 135 103; customer.service@macmillan.com.au

New Zealand agent/distributor: David Bateman Ltd, 30 Tarndale Grove, Off Bush Road, Albany, Auckland; tel. (09) 415 7664; fax (09) 415 8892

Ethical trading policy

At Anness Publishing we believe that business should be conducted in an ethical and ecologically sustainable way, with respect for the environment and a proper regard to the replacement of the natural resources we employ.

As a publisher, we use a lot of wood pulp to make high-quality paper for printing, and that wood commonly comes from spruce trees. We are therefore currently growing more than 500,000 trees in two Scottish forest plantations near Aberdeen – Berrymoss (130 hectares/320 acres) and West Touxhill (125 hectares/305 acres). The forests we manage contain twice the number of trees employed each year in paper-making for our books.

Because of this ongoing ecological investment programme, you, as our customer, can have the pleasure and reassurance of knowing that a tree is being cultivated on your behalf to naturally replace the materials used to make the book you are holding.

Our forestry programme is run in accordance with the UK Woodland Assurance Scheme (UKWAS) and will be certified by the internationally recognized Forest Stewardship Council (FSC). The FSC is a non-government organization dedicated to promoting responsible management of the world's forests. Certification ensures forests are managed in an environmentally sustainable and socially responsible way. For further information about this scheme, go to www.annesspublishing.com/trees

Publisher: Joanna Lorenz
Senior Managing Editor: Conor Kilgallon
Project Editor: Emma Clegg
Designer: Simon Daley
Illustrator: Robert Highton
Photography: William Lingwood
Food Stylist: Lucy McKelvie
Prop Stylist: Helen Trent
Production Controller: Pedro Nelson

Notes

Bracketed terms are for American readers.

For all recipes, quantities are given in both metric and imperial measures and, where appropriate, in standard cups and spoons. Follow one set of measures, but not a mixture, because they are not interchangeable.

Standard spoon and cup measures are level. 1 tsp = 5ml, 1 tbsp = 15ml, 1 cup = 250ml/8fl oz.

Australian standard tablespoons are 20ml. Australian readers should use 3 tsp in place of 1 tbsp for measuring small quantities.

American pints are 16fl oz/2 cups. American readers should use 20fl oz/2.5 cups in place of 1 pint when measuring liquids.

Electric oven temperatures in this book are for conventional ovens. When using a fan oven, the temperature will probably need to be reduced by about 10–20°C/20–40°F. Since ovens vary, you should check with your manufacturer's instruction book for guidance.

The nutritional analysis given for each recipe is calculated per portion (i.e. serving or item), unless otherwise stated. If the recipe gives a range, such as Serves 4–6, then the nutritional analysis will be for the smaller portion size, i.e. 6 servings. Measurements for sodium do not include salt added to taste.

Medium (US large) eggs are used unless otherwise stated.

Front cover shows Salted Salmon with Potatoes in Dill Sauce (see page 58); page 1 shows Lax Pudding (see page 56); page 2 shows Knäckebröd (see page 125); page 3 shows Rosehip Soup (see page 98).

Contents

Sweden: a personal introduction

I spent most of my childhood in Sweden, at my parents' home in central Stockholm and my aunt Brita's house in central Sweden. This gave me the experience of a mixture of city life, with particularly strong memories of the tempting attractions and smells of Osterrmalms hallen, *the famous food hall in Stockholm, as well as a life close to nature, fishing, collecting berries, making cream, and learning the secrets of planning and preparing Swedish food.*

I have a lasting childhood memory of sitting under the table in our kitchen enjoying the coming and going of people running back and forth. My parents were having what seemed to me like a banquet. I remember feeling transported by the smells of simmering stocks, the roasted meats and the baked bread. There were roasted pheasants and small fillets of roe deer, accompanied by fresh chanterelles and morel mushrooms used in perfectly prepared sauces. At other less hectic times I used to watch our cook Fanny in the kitchen, and over the years I learned from her the basics of Swedish cooking.

Every Christmas and every summer my parents took me to stay with my aunt Brita in Södermanland in central Sweden, an area full of beautiful manor houses and aristocratic homes with large expanses of land and lakes. While we were there I used to help make *gräddkarameller*, or Swedish fudge, by collecting milk from the dairy, making cream in a machine that separated the cream from the milk, and then boiling the cream with sugar until it changed colour and thickened. I also used to help in the kitchen by rolling meatballs, usually made from elk (moose).

While staying with my aunt I would often catch my own fish in the morning, in Lake Öljaren, next to Lake Hjälmaren. Perch was the easiest using just a worm and a cork, whereas for a pike you would need a spinner with good bait. Later in the day I would collect wild berries such as blueberries, strawberries and raspberries and pick chanterelles, ceps and parasol mushrooms in the woods. My aunt had a greenhouse and we picked cucumbers and pickled them with a solution of acetic acid, sugar and dill. In the garden there were always potatoes and dill to be collected, which are a divine combination.

Left The charming watercolours of Swedish artist Carl Larsson depict his family at their home in Sundborn, north-west of Stockholm. His paintings are associated with the traditional Sweden of the early 20th century.

Such close contact with nature is reflected in many of my recipes, in particular the Smoked Pike with Crème Fraîche and Chives where the fish is smoked in newspaper over an open fire. One summer, I was sailing with my parents in the Stockholm archipelago and we came across a little house where a lady was hanging out nets. My father asked if she had any fish to sell us and she showed us a pike swimming around in a large wooden box with holes in it, called a sump. The box was underwater and kept the fish alive and fresh. My father cooked it in the open air by salting it and then wrapping it in wet newspaper and cooking it over an open fire. My mother made a delicious fresh mayonnaise to go with it. The pike was the best I have ever eaten.

During this period Johan, a childhood friend, taught me how to make crayfish butter by crushing crayfish shells, adding unsalted butter, putting the mixture in boiling water and cooking it. The butter would float to the top and the shells would sink. This orange coloured butter was a delicious base for soups and sauces.

No food experience can be topped by the use of natural, fresh, seasonal produce and ingredients collected and caught in the local surroundings. Swedish recipes are characterized by natural ingredients and the selection of authentic recipes that follow are a part of this tradition.

Geography and climate

Sweden nestles between Norway and Finland, with the Baltic Sea and Gulf of Bothnia on the east and Skagerrak on the west. With cold, dark winters and hot, long summer days, Sweden's climate is extreme. In the Arctic north there are vast expanses of snow and complete silence and, in the winter, intense darkness, which is only broken by the fantastic northern lights that sparkle and dance across the polar skies in shades of red, green, blue and violet.

Despite Sweden being geographically the fourth largest country in Europe, the population has remained relatively small, at around nine million, and thinly spread. Over half of Sweden's land area is covered in forest and woodland; only seven per cent of the land is arable and just two per cent is grazing land, the latter all in the south. Wildlife such as elk (moose), reindeer (caribou), grouse and hare populate the forests and woodlands, and these are also home to many species of mushroom and native berries. The long coastline is dotted with numerous islands and there are around 95,000 lakes, where there are an amazing choice of 52 species of freshwater fish.

Sweden is traditionally divided into three major regions each of which have a number of provinces, 25 in total. Norrland, the largest region, in northern Sweden, includes the traditional provinces of Gästrikland, Hälsingland, Medelpad, Ångermanland, Västerbotten, Norrbotten, Härjedalen, Jämtland and Lappland. Svealand, the smallest region, is in central Sweden and includes the provinces of Uppland, Södermanland, Västmanland, Närke, Värmland and the southern parts

Above left Sweden is geographically Europe's fourth largest country. From north to south it has eight climatic zones.

Above right Jämtland, a province in the north of Sweden, has many mountains, plains and lakes and considerable snow in the winter.

of Dalarna. Götaland, or Götland, is the region of southern Sweden and includes the provinces of Dalsland, Västergötland, Östergötland, Småland, Öland, Gotland, Bohuslän, Skåne, Halland and Blekinge. Stockholm, the capital city, is built on 14 islands, between a large freshwater lake called Mälaren and the Baltic Sea. Stockholm is the most highly populated city with 750,000 inhabitants, followed by Gothenburg with 500,000 to the west and Malmö with 250,000 in the south. Because of the cold temperatures, the north is far less populated – Umeå is the largest northern city with 90,000 inhabitants.

Neighbouring countries

Among the surrounding Scandinavian regions Sweden has the most varied cuisine because of its range of agriculture and produce and because it embraces the dishes of neighbouring countries. Norway has a wild and mountainous terrain with a long coastline of deep fjords open to the Atlantic Ocean and consequently sea fish forms the staple diet, supplemented by reindeer (caribou). Denmark is low lying, green and lush and its produce is from fields and pastures with its agriculture orientated towards dairy produce, pork and potatoes. It is also renowned for its rich pastries. Finland is much closer to Sweden in terms of its terrain and climate, with much of the land covered in forests and freshwater lakes. So the main produce – pork, fish, potatoes, wild mushrooms and berries – is similar to that found in Sweden.

Right The river Dalälven in Dalarna, within the provinces of Norrland and Svealand, is one of many Swedish rivers popular for fishing.

Below The Kebnekaise Mountains in Swedish Lappland are round and low with flat tops and broad valleys.

Traditional festivals

Feasts and festivals play an important part in the Swedish calendar. Many of them are based on peasant traditions and are therefore closely associated with the changing seasons. Summer is celebrated with an understandable intensity – by a population who have endured a long, dark winter. Many of the traditional celebrations mentioned below are linked to the farming year, to the welcoming of spring, to the hunting and fishing seasons and to harvest time.

Shrove Tuesday

Recipes that regularly feature in the Shrove Tuesday celebrations at the end of February are roasted pork and Fat Tuesday buns (semla). These have a sweet overpowering almond flavour, intended as a celebratory, rich farewell to good food before the fasting regime of Lent began.

Our Lady's Day

On the 25th March farmers celebrate Vårfrudagen, or Our Lady's Day. Delicious waffles are made with a simple batter of an egg, a little flour and some cream or melted butter and sparkling water, which makes the waffles crispy. Some cooks even use snow if it is on the ground. Toppings for the waffles vary and include fried salty bacon or cloudberry jam and whipped cream.

Easter

Swedish legend has it that on Maundy Thursday witches would fly off on their broomsticks to a blue mountain where they would be entertained by the devil. So the tradition is that children dress up as witches, ride on broomsticks and visit their neighbours shouting "Glad Påsk" (Happy Easter) in return for treats. Halibut is often served on Good Friday, on the evening of Easter Saturday most Swedes will have a small smörgåsbord, and the Easter Sunday meal often

includes spinach soup and roasted lamb or pork with hasselback potatoes. It is also a good time to eat Nettle Soup with Egg Butterballs as the nettles are just coming up.

Valborgsmässa

Soon after Easter, Valborgsmässa is celebrated on the 1st May when the Swedes dance and sing to celebrate the end of winter and the coming of spring and summer. This is considered to be the beginning of summer even though it can still be very cold. The night before, huge bonfires made from juniper bushes are lit all over the country, and the smell creates a magical atmosphere.

Midsummer's Eve

This major Swedish festival takes place on the weekend nearest to 21st June. Traditionally everyone dances around a flower-bedecked maypole, folk songs are sung and folk music played. Midsummer's Eve is an all-night indulgence of dancing, eating and drinking, and the celebrations continue for almost 24 hours as it hardly gets dark at this time of year.

Right Dancers in folk costume in the Dalarna province of Sweden during the Midsummer's Eve celebrations.

The Crayfish Festival

During this August festival crayfish are cooked with dill, chilled and served in a large mound on a platter, garnished with fresh dill. The eating ritual is a happy, noisy affair. Paper lanterns are put up, jovial folk songs are sung and large paper napkins are provided for the diners. This dish is served with snaps or beer and toast and cheese flavoured with cumin and cloves.

Surströmming season

During this short season around August a strange and pungent dish called Surströmming is eaten – this Baltic herring dish from the north of Sweden dates back to the 16th century. The herring is salted and fermented in a large wooden barrel at room temperature for about six weeks and then canned. It is eaten with boiled potatoes and Tunnbröd, a thin soft bread, with butter and chopped raw onions. When the can is opened, the smell is unbearable, caused by the fermenting gas mixing with oxygen.

Nobel Prize dinner

Sweden is well known for the Nobel Prize, named after the famous scientist Alfred Nobel. The Nobel Prize dinner, a modern tradition, is held every year on 10th December and is an extraordinary feat of culinary skill. The first Nobelfest (Nobel Feast) was given in 1901, in the Mirrored Hall of the Grand Hotel in Stockholm. There were 150 guests and champagne and Russian caviar were

Right A traditional Swedish Christmas table loaded with cheese, bread, roast ham, marinated herring, beer and aquavit.

served. There were seven courses, which included crèpes fried in olive oil and fillet steak stuffed with foie gras. The dessert was an ice-cream bomb consisting of several different ice creams, or a tart filled with almond paste and topped with glazed fresh apricots. Nowadays, over 1000 guests attend the dinner, which is held at the Stockholm Town Hall.

The Day of Santa Lucia

At the end of the year, the Swedes celebrate light, for the long dark winters can induce a feeling of melancholy. The Day of Santa Lucia, the Queen of Light, falls on the 13th December. A young girl (or several young girls) is chosen to represent the saint and wear a crown of candles in her hair, although these days they are usually electric. After the procession, coffee is served with Lucia Saffron Buns and Gingerbread Biscuits.

Christmas

The Day of Santa Lucia marks the beginning of the magical Christmas season. The climax is Christmas Eve (Julafton), when smörgåsbord is served at lunchtime. A Christmas ham glazed with mustard and breadcrumbs is the centrepiece and other traditional Christmas dishes include Glassblower's herrings, pork sausage, potatoes and vört bread. The meal ends with coffee and Christmas cookies. In the evening, dishes include lutfisk, a speciality of both Sweden and Norway, which is a dish with a jelly-like consistency made from dried cod or ling soaked in a lye solution and then boiled. It is served with a white sauce, melted butter, peas, new potatoes and mustard. Dessert is typically julgröt, Sweden's traditional creamed rice pudding, which has a lucky almond hidden inside, a sign of marriage or great fortune. Some Swedes make their julgröt more traditionally using barley instead of rice.

Left A Day of Santa Lucia celebration at a church in Kekvattnet, Värmland, in the central Svealand province of Sweden.

Livestock and produce

The open and cultivated landscapes in Sweden are home to a range of domestic animals and crops, from chickens and pigs to potatoes and corn. Dairy farms are common, although their numbers have decreased in recent years, and there is an associated emphasis on milk, cream, butter and cheese products. The country's many deep forests and wetlands have a variety of wild animals and game, as well as the mushrooms and wild berries that feature largely in the diet.

Wild and domestic animals

The far north of Sweden lies within the Arctic Circle, and it is on its bleak mountains and moorlands, as in neighbouring Finland and Norway, that most reindeer (caribou) are farmed. Many of the most exquisite and exotic Swedish meat delicacies come from northern Sweden, such as smoked reindeer fillet and grouse. Further south, in the large expanses of forest and woodland, reindeer, elk (moose), bear, lynx, hare and beaver roam.

The hunting of hare, elk, and reindeer, as well as grouse, is a popular sport, particularly in the north of Sweden, although it is strictly policed and hunters require gun licences and training. Reindeer are free to roam widely but are reared on farms, unlike the elk (moose), which is always wild. Access to both hunting and fishing in Sweden is dependent on the locality as well as the distance to the coast or forests. Hunters tend to focus on deer and elk (moose), which both form a natural and integral part of the Swedish cuisine. Pork is a staple food, particularly in the south, and wild boar has recently been introduced as an animal for hunting enthusiasts, which means it can now be found in the Stockholm markets.

Many delicious sausages, similar to salamis, are also produced, including the pricki korv, the popular onsala korv and skånsk senap, which is flavoured with strong sweet wholegrain mustard. There is also a sausage unique to Sweden called isterband that contains oatmeal, which is slowly poached and then grilled.

Cows and sheep graze in the meadows and pastures, resulting in a variety of dairy products, particularly cheese, and a regular supply of excellent lamb and beef. Veal is eaten regularly and restaurants often serve veal sweetbreads (from the pancreas), which are a Swedish speciality. Swedish farmers have a reputation for good-quality organic farming: cattle are not fed on offal pellets, and intensive and factory farming techniques are not encouraged for any animals. This standard reduces the stress on the animals while they are alive and means that the meat and poultry is disease-free. Chickens are commonly kept, but while they are eaten, generally other birds, such as grouse or geese, are preferred. Chickens are valued in Sweden mainly for their eggs.

A taste of wild meat

♦ Venison is the name for deer meat, which can be roe deer, red deer, fallow deer or reindeer (caribou). Its flesh is dark red, lean and has a gamey flavour.
♦ Reindeer is a small deer and in Sweden it is eaten fresh, smoked and dried. It is also delicately salted and cold smoked to preserve it.
♦ The elk (moose), or älg in Swedish, is a member of the deer family, and eats only moss. It is hunted in Sweden and the meat has very little fat, but a rich, fine flavour that differs from all other venison. It is hunted in the autumn and eaten between November and March.
♦ The most sought-after wild meat delicacies are reindeer heart, smoked elk (moose) heart and elk thigh.

Above Reindeer (caribou) are most at home in colder temperatures, and are farmed mainly in the north of Sweden.

Fish and seafood

The seas that surround Sweden provide a wealth of sea fish and shellfish and the lakes and rivers are a rich source of freshwater fish. In fact, the settlement of the Swedish population focused on the fishing areas on the east coast around present-day Stockholm, and on the west coast around present-day Gothenburg.

Saltwater fishing from the west coast provides cod, haddock and salmon, while Baltic herring, pike, perch and zander are plentiful in the Stockholm archipelago, one of the biggest of the Baltic Sea.

Freshwater crayfish, a popular ingredient in the Swedish diet, are caught in the lakes and rivers. Arctic char are caught in Lake Vättern. Laveret, bleak and whitefish can only be caught in the rivers in the north of Sweden, as well as the Gulf of Bothnia, the northern part of the Baltic Sea.

Swedish fish and shellfish have a reputation in the food industry for their rich flavours and fine consistency, a result of natural, slow growth in cold, clear waters. Fish roe is used widely in Swedish cuisine, especially trout and salmon roe, and a smoked cod roe called kalles kaviar is popular with children. Whitefish has a delicious orange roe known as löjrom, which is as prized in Sweden as caviar is in Russia.

Crops

The long dark Swedish winters meant that fresh vegetables were scarce and traditional recipes relied on preserved ones. Many of these are still popular today. In the past, root vegetables such as turnips and the native rutabaga (or swede), which kept well during the winter, became key ingredients. They then gradually became supplanted by the potato in the 18th century.

The more fertile soil in the south favours arable farming. This is where the potato, much loved by the local population, is grown, along with other vegetable crops such as beetroot (beet), cabbage, kale, carrots, corn, leeks, broccoli, cucumber and peas. Barley, wheat, rye and oats are also grown, as well as oilseed rape and sugar beet.

The Swedes are very conscientious about their diet and have strict regulations on how crops are grown and what fertilizers are used. The use of chemical pesticides and artificial fertilizers has been dramatically reduced, by about 70 per cent, over the past ten years, and antibiotics may only be given to farm animals in the event of disease. In the winter months Swedish soil is allowed to rest and recover, in many areas under a protective covering of snow.

Above, left to right Gravlax, or thin slices of salmon cured in salt, sugar and dill; anchovies are a popular ingredient in Swedish dishes; Baltic or Bismarck herring is found only in the Baltic Sea.

Dairy produce

Because of the emphasis on dairy farming, dairy products play a crucial role. Milk, cream and butter form the basis of many delicious desserts, and creamy pastries and cheese are eaten in large quantities. In the past, most people relied on preserved foods, and drinking fresh milk or eating fresh butter and eggs was a rare pleasure; home-produced butter and eggs were usually sold to the wealthy. Milk was fermented or preserved with the aid of bacterial cultures, creating yogurt-like soured milks (including filmjölk and stringy långfil), curdled milk (filbunke) or sour cream (gräddfil), and these are all still popular. It was also made into cheese.

The country boasts almost 200 different cheeses, most of which are semi-soft, and these are made from cow's, sheep's or goat's milk. Cheese made from caramelized whey is unique to Sweden and Norway, and the Swedish variety is called Mesost. It is a sweet goat's milk cheese, which is brown and has a creamy sweet chocolatey flavour with a bitter aftertaste. For breakfast the Swedes usually eat a soft cheese such as Kvark or yogurt, and for lunch they will invariably have cheese, in a sandwich or served with pickled herrings.

Västerbotten, sometimes called "Swedish Parmesan", is a semi-hard cheese similar in flavour to a very strong English Cheddar or Italian Reggiano Parmesan, and is considered by many to be the best Swedish cheese. Hushållsost is a semi-hard cheese made from whole cow's milk with a mild, slightly sour taste, and is a common favourite. Other semi-soft cheeses include Grevé, which resembles Swiss Emmenthal with a sweet mild flavour; Prästost, a fine old Swedish cheese with a strong sharp fruity flavour when well matured; and Sveciaost, which has a mild flavour that becomes strong and sharp when aged. Sveciaost is sometimes sold flavoured with cloves, caraway or cumin. Kryddost is a hard cheese flavoured with caraway and cloves. A popular blue cheese is Adelost and an excellent blue cheese, made from sheep's milk in southern Götaland, is Wanås.

Mushrooms

Wild mushrooms are plentiful in Sweden and locals have a passion for gathering and eating them. Good places to find mushrooms are jealously guarded secrets among both serious collectors and casual harvesters of porcini mushrooms (also known as cep meaning king of mushrooms) and chanterelles.

The most highly regarded mushroom is the chanterelle, which is usually served with a piece of meat, or simply fried with a cream sauce and some onions and served in a sandwich. Sweden also has a reputation for good porcini mushrooms. Famous for their flavour and smell, many tonnes of them are exported each year.

Wild berries and fruits

Berries are widely available throughout Sweden and, when in season, you will find many people in the woods gathering them. Varieties include bilberries, cloudberries, buckthorn and lingonberries as well as strawberries, blackberries and raspberries. They are all very high in vitamin C, especially lingonberries. Cloudberries, amber-coloured raspberry-sized berries, are the rarest variety and only come from the north of Sweden. Lingonberries, however, tiny, tart red berries that belong to the cranberry family, can be found all over Sweden and are exported abroad. Most lingonberries are preserved as a sauce or jam, when they are simply stirred with sugar and then put straight into jars – their citric

acid content is so high that they need no cooking. They are delicious served with wild meats such as elk (moose) and roe deer, but frequently the lingonberry preserve is served with meatballs. The use of lingonberry jam in Swedish cooking was important traditionally, since it provided a source of vitamin C during the winter. It also added some freshness to the food of the past, which could be rather heavy. It is still a favourite today.

Bilberries, or blåbär as the Swedish call them, grow in the same woodland areas as lingonberries. They are like a small version of the cultivated blueberry and are good for making into jam or using in sweet pies. The Swedes also make a bilberry soup and a rosehip soup, both of which are popular desserts and can also be eaten at breakfast time with yogurt. Berries such as raspberries, blueberries and wild strawberries are also used to make a delectable fruit compote that is called drottningkräm.

Below, left to right The porcini or cep mushroom is a favourite in Sweden; rosehips are used to make the popular dessert Rosehip Soup; collecting cloudberries, which are eaten fresh as well as featuring in delicious desserts and preserves.

The Swedish diet

Because of the extreme climate, the traditional Swedish approach to eating emphasized the need to preserve and store the fresh produce obtained in the warmer months and so make it last throughout the year. As a result the diet was characterized by plain, nutritious dishes that use these stored ingredients. Despite modern refrigeration techniques, these preserved ingredients still provide the backbone of the diet.

Traditionally, people would gather all that they needed during the summer harvest, preserve it and then save it for future use in the darker, less productive times of year. Even eating fresh berries was a real treat, because berries were collected and then cooked into jam for use during the winter. Fresh vegetables were another rare luxury, since there was always a pressure to preserve or pickle them. It was the same story with potatoes and other root vegetables, which used to be stacked away in an earth cellar for winter use.

Husmanskost and healthy eating
Swedish home cooking, or husmanskost, was born from the need for such food preservation techniques and is often based on traditional methods of smoking, fermenting, salting, drying, marinating and poaching ingredients such as seafood, poultry, lamb, beef, veal and wild game. Husmanskost consists of plain, rustic dishes and familiar classics include meatballs, stuffed cabbage rolls and yellow pea soup. The husmanskost is still a strong contemporary tradition and forms the main component of the Swedish smörgåsbord.

In more recent times the best of the traditional recipes have been modernized so that they are less hearty and simpler to prepare, and also in keeping with today's lifestyles and different nutritional needs. Fresh fruit and vegetables have been added, traditional fatty dishes have been replaced with steaks and stews,

Above left A variety of seafood and vegetables in a small market in Stockholm.

Above right A Christmas buffet on display at Stallmästaregarden, which is Stockholm's oldest hotel and restaurant.

stocks are reduced to give deliciously flavoured jus or gravy, and sauces have been made lighter and created with less cream – but although their fat content has been reduced, none of their other characteristics have been lost. Also, the large quantities of oil-rich salmon and herrings that the Swedes eat have always contained high amounts of the essential polyunsaturated fats called omega-3 fatty acids, which are an invaluable source of vitamins and are essential to good health.

Eating patterns

The daily dietary regime in Sweden is based around three main meals. Breakfast usually consists of open sandwiches with hard cheese or slices of meat, and possibly crispbread (knäckebröd). Swedes don't use sweet spreads on their breads but the traditional Swedish bread, sirapslimpa, is sweetened in itself, and is baked with syrup. Yogurt and fermented milk (filmjölk) are common breakfast foods, and are usually served in a bowl with cereals such as cornflakes or muesli (granola), sometimes with sugar, fruit or jam. Porridge (gröt) is another popular breakfast food often made of rolled oats, and eaten with milk and fruit or jam.

Lunch tends to be a light snack such as a sandwich whereas the evening meal is usually hot. At the table, Swedes like to

Below Strandvägen is an exclusive boulevard in the Östermalm area of Stockholm – it has many restaurants that overlook the waterfront.

serve themselves unless it is impractical, and it is therefore considered polite to finish what one has served oneself.

Smörgåsbord

The most well-known eating style in Sweden is the smörgåsbord, or bread-and-butter table. There was a distinguishable smörgåsbord tradition as far back as the 16th century, when all the food for a meal would be placed on the table at the same time. At the beginning the smörgåsbord dishes were simple, consisting of bread, butter, cheese and herring but as the custom continued, more and more dishes were added. By the 18th century it had become a regular feature in most homes.

The smörgåsbord is commonly prepared for special occasions such as Christmas, Easter and midsummer. On these occasions, the array of food is set out on a long table and people continue to help themselves.

Swedish smörgåsbord

Recipe ideas that could be included in a formal smörgåsbord are shown below.

Chilled fish dishes
Mustard Herrings (Senap sill)
Gravlax with Mustard and Dill Sauce (Gravlax med gravlax sås)
Salted Salmon with Béchamel and Dill (Rimmad lax med dillstuvad potatis)

Savoury dishes
West Coast Salad (Västkust salad)
Hare Pâté (Har pâté)
Christmas Ham with Swedish Mustard (Julskinka med senap)
Anchovy Terrine (Gubbröra)
Västerbotten Cheese Flan (Västerbotten ost flan)

Hot dishes
Stuffed Cabbage Rolls (Kåldomar)
Elk Meatballs with Lingon (Alg köttbullar med lingon)
Jansson's Temptation (Jansson's frestelse)
Swedish Hash (Pytt-i-panna)

Desserts
Rice porridge (Risgrynsgröt)
Wild Berry Tart (Skogshär flan)
Almond Stuffed Baked Apples (Drottningäpplen)
Gingerbread Biscuits (Pepparkakor)

Diners start with a selection of herring, such as Glasmästarsill, or other fish and shellfish dishes. These are served with boiled potatoes, hard-boiled eggs and bread, and accompanied by snaps. They then proceed to cold, savoury dishes such as cuts of game, poultry and meat, pâtés and salads and then hot dishes, such as the traditional Jansson's Temptation. Sweet desserts are served last, usually with coffee. Every time diners choose their next selection, they change their plate so that the flavours do not intermingle. Diners may return to the table as often as they wish but they must not load their plate with too many foods at the same time.

Because preparing a full smörgåsbord involves considerable work, it is unusual to experience the real smörgåsbord anywhere other than in restaurants, on festival days or on special occasions.

Swedish bread
Rye bread was traditionally baked slowly into durable dark loaves or alternatively dried into hard crispbread (knäckebröd) or rusks (skorpor) that could be stored for long periods. The knäckebröd flat breads are made with rye flour and are often flavoured with cumin. One of the rye

breads is a delicious bread called kavring, with allspice and caraway added, which is wonderful with smoked fish, especially smoked eel. Rågbröd is a traditional Swedish rye bread, made in large flat loaves and often containing molasses. Limpa is another Swedish favourite – a leavened rye loaf, sweetened with molasses or honey, flavoured with orange and spiced with cardamon, cumin, fennel and anise seeds. Vört limpa is a darker loaf than limpa, with a greater proportion of rye together with the molasses and orange rind, which is either grated or finely chopped. In spite of the sweet molasses, the dark loaf is intended to be eaten with soft cheese or salted herring.

Another sweet bread is Swedish cardamom bread, a spicy fruit bread with white flour. There is also a half-sweet, half-savoury white bread called caraway bread, made with a little sugar and butter and a subtle savoury flavour. Krisprolls are also popular, eaten at almost any time of the day, but particularly at breakfast. They are baked until entirely crisp and have a noticeably sweet flavour.

Fika and sweet treats
In apparent contradiction to the preserved element of the main diet, Swedish cookies, cakes, buns, pastries

Above, left to right *Knäckebröd* is a crispbread made with rolled oats; *vört limpa* is a festive bread flavoured with warm spices and fresh orange; Lucia Saffron Buns are eaten to celebate Saint Lucia Day.

and desserts are full of rich ingredients. Pastries ooze with cream, chocolate and jam, cakes and desserts are filled with almond paste or marzipan fillings, and other common sweet favourites include meringues, curd cakes and apple pies, all served with creamy vanilla sauces.

One of the most important customs in Sweden is fika or kaffe med bakelser (coffee with pastries). The social routine of fika seems to dominate Swedish everyday life and is considered a social necessity for meeting and greeting those you meet in the course of your day. Traditionally cakes and sweetmeats for fika are prepared when you are expecting guests, and the more important the guest, the more grand the selection of cakes.

Summer is the season for the strawberry and cream cake. Apple cakes arrive in the late summer and autumn and are served with vanilla custard, ice cream or whipped cream. In the winter, treats include knäck, a Christmas toffee; ischoklad or cold ice-chocolate toffees; the Lucia Saffron Bun or lussekatt, eaten on 13 December for the Saint Lucia celebration; the ginger snap or pepparkakor; and the Lenten bun or semla, a cream-filled wheat bun eaten before Lent. Pancakes, muffins, sponge cakes and different sorts of cookies and pies – such as apple, blueberry and rhubarb – are typical desserts, almost always served with coffee.

Herbs, spices and seasonings

Many years ago a lack of available spices made Swedish food rather plain, although local herbs and plants such as dill, parsley, marjoram and thyme have been used since ancient times. Before the imports of new herbs and spices, one of the main ways of adding flavour was with salt, which was used extensively in preserving. Sugar was also used in this way but this was a later addition brought over from the West Indies. It was expensive and so used sparingly, but now it is cheap and is used in pickling fish.

Over the years the Swedes have incorporated various exotic spices and plants in their cuisine that were introduced to Sweden in the 17th century by ships returning from the West Indies. Cardamom, cinnamon and ginger are all spices that now form a crucial part of Swedish traditional cooking. Saffron is also a favourite, used all the year round in the Saffron Pancake from Gotland and in Lucia Saffron Buns. Another spice often added to Swedish bread, especially rye bread, is caraway and this is also used to flavour cheese.

Other important herbs and spices in the contemporary Swedish kitchen are nutmeg, cloves, bay leaves, mustard, pepper (especially white), juniper berries and chervil. All the commonly used spices give vibrant rather than hot and garlicky tastes.

Alcoholic drinks

Historically, the Swedes have been a nation of beer drinkers rather than wine drinkers because the Swedish climate is not suitable for grape cultivation. Beer also complements Swedish food very well. Nevertheless, Swedes are great wine lovers and import large quantities.

A popular Swdish drink is a spirit called aquavit, which means water of life in Latin, also referred to as snaps or brännvin, which in Swedish means fiery wine. This colourless drink is made with potato or grain spirits and tastes rather like vodka, which is drunk in most Eastern European countries. Its bitter flavour in combination with the alcohol, like beer, complements the traditional rich Swedish foods and it also stimulates the appetite. This drink enhances cold dishes and is an excellent accompaniment to pickled herring or gravlax. Normally aquavit is drunk chilled, and it is a regular feature at the smörgåsbord table. Herbs and spices, such as caraway or cumin, are added to aquavit, and these contribute to the drink's colour and flavour. Aquavit has many different flavours in Sweden and these depend on its exact place of origin.

Punsch is a liqueur exclusive to Sweden and is made from an Indian spice called arrak. It is very sweet and the tradition used to be to serve it warm with the traditional Yellow Pea Soup. The flavour is not dissimilar to rum but much sweeter. Hot Pepper Liquorice Vodka is another popular drink, which is often drunk at nightclubs in Stockholm, and was created originally by the addition of Turkish pepper liquorice sweets to a bottle of vodka.

Below, left to right Fresh dill flavours Swedish dishes such as gravlax; cinnamon is a more recently introduced spice, but is now a favourite; juniper berries are seen as an essential spice to accompany the flavours of red meat, particularly venison.

Appetizers & side dishes

Yellow pea soup

Nettle soup with
　egg butterballs

Lacy potato pancakes

West coast salad

Toast skagen

Grilled goat's cheese
　with baby beetroot

Mustard herrings

Sunny-eye anchovies

Curried herrings

Hare pâté

Anchovy terrine

Smoked eel with
　scrambled eggs

Västerbotten cheese flan

Gravlax with mustard
　and dill sauce

Stuffed cabbage rolls

Herring bites and
cheesy grills

It has become increasingly fashionable in the restaurant world to serve food using a selection of small dishes. More and more venues now serve "grazing menus", similar to the Spanish tapas and the Greek meze. Swedish food is perfectly suited to this way of eating and the smörgåsbord is a classic example. All guests can help themselves from a buffet to many small, light savoury dishes, all freshly made, and often served with a vast array of cheeses such as Kryddost, Cheddar, Grevé and Sveciaost.

Many of the Swedish appetizers and light dishes rely on fish, the Gravlax with Mustard and Dill Sauce as a classic treatment of salted salmon being the most famous. As well as other examples of light fish dishes, such as Mustard Herrings (Senaps sill) and Smoked Eel with Scrambled Eggs, you will also find a delicious Västerbotten Cheese Flan, warming soups, such as the Yellow Pea Soup (Ärtsoppa), and some delicious light dishes such as Toast Skagen (Skagenröra) and Grilled Goat's Cheese with Baby Beetroot.

Use this chapter as a way of experimenting with the combined taste of several different dishes and impress your guests with a selection of small dishes in a smörgåsbord style.

Yellow pea soup
Ärtsoppa

In the Middle Ages, this soup was always served on Thursdays to prepare the population for the Christian weekend fast that started on Friday. Following this ancient tradition, the soup would be served on a Thursday in the army and navy. In the middle of the 16th century, King Erik XIV of Sweden was famously assassinated by his ambitious brothers, who put poison in his bowl of Yellow Pea Soup!

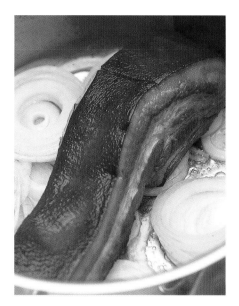

Serves 6–8

500g/1¼lb yellow split peas

30ml/2 tbsp vegetable oil

1 Spanish (Bermuda) onion, sliced

500g/1¼lb/2¾ cups salted pork belly or bacon

2 litres/3½ pints/8 cups water or ham stock

bay leaf

1 bunch thyme sprigs

5ml/1 tsp chopped fresh thyme and/or marjoram

Swedish mustard, to serve

1 Soak the yellow split peas in cold water overnight. The next day, drain them and put to one side.

2 Heat the oil in a large, heavy pan, add the onion and pork belly and when browned, add the water or ham stock. Heat until simmering then skim off any foam and cook for about 1 hour.

3 Add the peas, bay leaf and thyme sprigs and leave to cook for about a further hour until the peas are soft and the pork is cooked and falling apart.

4 Remove the pork from the pan and cut it into cubes, then return it to the pan with the fresh thyme and/or marjoram.

5 Season the soup with salt to taste before serving, although because the meat is salty, the soup may not need extra seasoning. Serve the soup with Swedish mustard and a hard bread such as rye bread or Knäckebröd.

Cook's tips

• Often served as a main course, this soup is traditionally served with hot Swedish punsch (a strong liqueur with arrack), followed by pancakes with strawberry jam and cream.
• Swedes dip their spoons into the mustard before taking a spoonful of soup. Any mild mustard can be used as a substitute.

Per portion Energy 374kcal/1569kJ; Protein 25.8g; Carbohydrate 38.3g, of which sugars 3.7g; Fat 14g, of which saturates 4.3g; Cholesterol 33mg; Calcium 57mg; Fibre 3.9g; Sodium 988mg.

a knob (pat) of butter

1 onion, roughly chopped

225g/8oz nettles (top 4 leaves from each plant only) or young spinach leaves

600ml/1 pint/2½ cups chicken stock

30ml/2 tbsp sherry

150ml/¼ pint/⅔ cup double (heavy) cream

5ml/½ tsp freshly grated nutmeg

salt and ground black pepper

For the butterballs

115g/4oz/½ cup butter

2 hard-boiled egg yolks

salt and ground black pepper

Nettle soup with egg butterballs
Näselsoppa med ägg

Nettle soup is extremely nutritious but as nettles cannot be found all year around, as an alternative you can use spinach, which goes equally well with the butterballs. The use of nettles is common throughout northern Europe, including Sweden, where they grow more prolifically than in hotter countries.

1 First make the butterballs. Put the butter and hard-boiled egg yolks in a bowl and mash together. Season the mixture with salt and pepper to taste. Roll into balls approximately 2cm/1in in diameter and chill in the refrigerator until ready to serve.

2 To make the soup, melt the butter in a saucepan, add the onion and fry until softened. Add the nettles or spinach, stir in the stock and season with salt and pepper. Bring to the boil then cook over a medium heat for 1 minute.

3 Pour the soup into a food processor and whiz until roughly chopped. Return to the pan, add the sherry, stir in the cream and sprinkle with nutmeg. Heat gently until warm but do not allow the soup to boil. Serve in warmed bowls with the butterballs bobbing on the surface and just beginning to melt.

Per portion Energy 239kcal/982kJ; Protein 2g; Carbohydrate 1.5g, of which sugars 1.3g; Fat 24.5g, of which saturates 14.8g; Cholesterol 109mg; Calcium 68mg; Fibre 0.7g; Sodium 141mg.

Lacy potato pancakes
Råraka

These pretty, lacy pancakes should be served as an accompaniment to a fish dish or smoked salmon. In Sweden, small ones are often served as canapés at parties. They're also good served as an appetizer, topped with smoked salmon, crème fraîche or sour cream, and chopped red onion.

1 Peel and grate the potatoes. Put in a bowl, add the leek and carrot, if using, and mix them all together.

2 Heat the butter and oil in a frying pan and when smoking, add spoonfuls of the potato mixture to make 7.5cm/3in pancakes. Fry the pancakes, turning once, until golden brown on both sides. Season with salt and pepper and serve hot.

Per portion Energy 182kcal/767kJ; Protein 3.9g; Carbohydrate 33.1g, of which sugars 3.3g; Fat 4.6g, of which saturates 1.8g; Cholesterol 5mg; Calcium 20mg; Fibre 2.7g; Sodium 38mg.

Serves 6

6 large potatoes

1 leek, finely sliced

1 carrot, grated (optional)

15g/$\frac{1}{2}$oz butter

15ml/1 tbsp vegetable oil

salt and ground black pepper

Cook's tip Once the air gets to them, grated potatoes tend to turn brown. So either avoid preparing them too far in advance of cooking, or put the grated potato in a bowl of water, which helps to stop oxidation.

Serves 6–8

200g/7oz fresh asparagus spears

1 kg/2¼lb shell-on cooked prawns (shrimp)

200g/7oz can mussels in brine

100g/3½oz can crab meat in brine or the meat from 2 large cooked crabs

200g/7oz small mushrooms, sliced

1 cos or romaine lettuce

For the dressing

105ml/7 tbsp mayonnaise

5ml/1 tsp tomato purée (paste)

pinch of salt

1 garlic clove, crushed

15ml/1 tbsp chopped fresh dill

For the garnish

1 potato

vegetable oil, for deep-frying

4 baby tomatoes, quartered

2 lemons, cut into wedges

1 bunch fresh dill

Cook's tip For a luxurious touch to this dish, try adding some lobster.

West coast salad
Västkust salad

After its fashionable popularity in the 1960s this crustacean salad has now become a stylish classic in Sweden. The west coast, from where it originates, abounds with fresh seafood, as well as picturesque fishing villages such as Smögen and Grebbestad. The dish is delicious served with cold beer.

1 Stand the asparagus spears upright in a deep pan or put in an asparagus pan, pour in enough boiling water to come three-quarters of the way up the stalks and simmer for about 10 minutes until tender. Drain and, when cool enough to handle, cut into 5cm/2in lengths.

2 Carefully remove the shells from the prawns, keeping them intact. If using canned fish, drain the brine from the mussels and crab then carefully mix the prawns with the mussels, crab meat, asparagus and mushrooms.

3 To make the potato garnish, very finely grate the potato and rinse under cold running water to wash off the starch. Put the potato on a clean dish towel and pat dry. Heat the oil in a deep-fryer or pan to 180–190°C/350–375°F or until a cube of bread browns in 30 seconds. Add the grated potato and fry until golden brown then remove from the pan with a slotted spoon. Drain on kitchen paper and leave to cool.

4 To make the dressing, mix together the mayonnaise, tomato purée, salt, garlic and dill. Add the dressing to the fish mixture and carefully mix together so that the prawns and mussels remain whole.

5 To serve the salad, chop the lettuce very finely and place on individual plates. Place the salad on the chopped lettuce and garnish with the fried potato, tomatoes, lemon wedges and dill.

Per portion Energy 594kcal/2531kJ; Protein 113.3g; Carbohydrate 2.8g, of which sugars 1.2g; Fat 14.6g, of which saturates 2.9g; Cholesterol 1337mg; Calcium 565mg; Fibre 0.9g; Sodium 7723mg.

Toast skagen
Skagenröra

This dish originates from the west coast of Sweden, between Sweden and Denmark. Skagenröra, which translates as "a mixture from the sea", is often served in restaurants as a tasty seafood snack. You can use peeled prawns, but those with their shell on taste and look better.

1 Carefully remove the shells from the prawns, keeping them intact. Put the sour cream, mayonnaise, chopped dill, chives and lemon juice in a large bowl. Season with salt and pepper to taste then stir in the prawns.

2 Melt the butter in a large frying pan, add the bread slices and fry until golden brown on both sides.

3 Serve the prawn mixture piled on top of the fried bread and garnish with a small amount of the lumpfish roe and a frond of dill.

Per portion Energy 415kcal/1726kJ; Protein 14.5g; Carbohydrate 15.2g, of which sugars 2.5g; Fat 33.4g, of which saturates 9.2g; Cholesterol 180mg; Calcium 128mg; Fibre 0.7g; Sodium 1065mg.

Serves 6–8

1kg/2¼lb shell-on cooked prawns (shrimp)

250ml/8fl oz/1 cup sour cream

250ml/8fl oz/1 cup thick mayonnaise

30ml/2 tbsp chopped fresh dill plus fronds, to garnish

30ml/2 tbsp chopped fresh chives

a squeeze of lemon juice

25–50g/1–2oz/2–4 tbsp butter

8 slices bread, halved

5ml/1 tsp red lumpfish roe

salt and ground black pepper

Cook's tip Salmon roe is ideal to use as a garnish, as its beautiful orange colour and large eggs makes the dish look rather special. Grated horseradish is another good accompaniment.

Serves 6

6 small raw beetroots (beets)

6 slices French bread

6 slices (250g/9oz) goat's cheese

30ml/2 tbsp walnut oil

salt and ground black pepper

Grilled goat's cheese with baby beetroot
Färsk getost med rödbetor och valnötsolja

Beetroots are considered a delicacy when they are freshly dug out of the ground in early summer. In Sweden they are usually served with whipped butter, called "primör". This recipe adds a new dimension to the beetroot and the goat's cheese marries well with its sweetness.

1 Cook the beetroots in boiling salted water for 40 minutes until tender. Leave to cool slightly then remove the skin and slice the beetroots.

2 Toast the French bread slices on both sides. Arrange the beetroot slices in a fan on the toasted bread then place a slice of goat's cheese on top of each.

3 Place the slices on a grill (broiler) pan and grill (broil) until the cheese has melted and is golden brown. Serve immediately, drizzled with a little walnut oil and black pepper ground on top.

Per portion Energy 290kcal/1215kJ; Protein 13.3g; Carbohydrate 26.7g, of which sugars 5g; Fat 15.2g, of which saturates 7.9g; Cholesterol 39mg; Calcium 114mg; Fibre 1.9g; Sodium 530mg.

Herring selection

In Sweden, herrings form an essential part of the diet and, as an oily fish rich in vitamin D, they have welcome health benefits. They can be served in many different ways and here are three suggestions – Curried Herrings (see left, back dish), Mustard Herrings (see left, middle dish) and Sunny-eye Anchovies (see left, front dish), made with the smallest member of the herring family. The Mustard Herrings need to be marinated for 10–12 hours, but the others can be quickly prepared for entertaining unexpected guests.

Mustard herrings
Senap sill

1 To prepare the herrings, cut off the head and fins. Make a slit down the belly and remove the guts. Rinse under cold water and pat dry on kitchen paper. Put the fish, skin side up, on a board and with the heel of your hand press down firmly to loosen the backbone. Turn the fish over, cut the backbone near the head and then remove. Finally, pull off the skin down towards the tail, being careful not to break the flesh.

2 In a large, shallow dish, mix the water and vinegar together and place the fish fillets in the mixture. Leave to marinate in the refrigerator for 10–12 hours.

3 Drain the marinade and dry the fish on kitchen paper. To make the sauce, mix the mayonnaise, mustard, sugar and dill together in the cleaned shallow dish. Add the fish and leave in the refrigerator for a further day. Garnish with dill fronds and serve with boiled new potatoes.

Per portion Energy 381kcal/1582kJ; Protein 26.7g; Carbohydrate 3.2g, of which sugars 3g; Fat 29.1g, of which saturates 5.7g; Cholesterol 68mg; Calcium 133mg; Fibre 0.6g; Sodium 479mg.

Serves 4

750g/1lb 10oz fresh small herrings or large sardines

350ml/12fl oz/1$\frac{1}{2}$ cups water

75ml/5 tbsp white vinegar

fresh dill fronds, to garnish

boiled new potatoes, to serve

For the mustard sauce

75ml/5 tbsp mayonnaise

25ml/1$\frac{1}{2}$ tbsp French wholegrain mustard

7.5ml/1$\frac{1}{2}$ tsp caster (superfine) sugar

60ml/4 tbsp chopped fresh dill

Cook's tip Herrings have been a staple food source, especially for northern Europeans, from 3000 BC, and pickled herring is one of the most popular Scandinavian dishes. Pickled herring is commonly served with dark rye bread, crisp bread or potatoes as well as a glass of snaps. A selection of pickled herring dishes is essential during Christmas and Midsummer celebrations.

Sunny-eye anchovies
Solöga

1 Chop the anchovies and put them in the centre of a serving dish. Then arrange the onion in a ring around the anchovies, followed by a ring of capers and then a ring of chopped beetroot.

2 Cut a nick in the shell of each egg and open up the lid you have created. Pour away the white and return the yolk to the shell. Place the raw egg yolks in their shell in the middle of the dish.

3 Alternatively, mix all the ingredients together, season with ground black pepper, and serve on crispbread.

Per portion Energy 86kcal/357kJ; Protein 8g; Carbohydrate 1.6g, of which sugars 1.3g; Fat 5.3g, of which saturates 1.2g; Cholesterol 117mg; Calcium 92mg; Fibre 0.4g; Sodium 997mg.

Serves 4

100g/3½ oz can Swedish anchovies (see cook's tip on page 34)

1 red onion, finely chopped

15ml/1 tbsp small capers

15ml/1 tbsp chopped pickled beetroot (beet)

2 egg yolks

crispbread, to serve

Cook's note Herrings have a high nutritional value. They contain protein and give the essential amino acids that the body needs. They also provide vitamins A, B, D, E and minerals including iron and phosphorus. They contain polyunsaturated fats and overall are low in calories.

Curried herrings
Currysill

1 Start by cutting the matjes fillets into 1cm/½in pieces. Then cube the cold boiled potatoes and chop the hard-boiled eggs.

2 Stir the curry powder into the mayonnaise. Then add the fish, potatoes and hard-boiled eggs and mix them together. Leave in the refrigerator for about 15 minutes to chill. Garnish the herrings with parsley and dill and serve with crispbread.

Serves 4

150g/5oz jar matjes herrings

3–4 cold, boiled new potatoes

2 hard-boiled eggs

5ml/1 tsp curry powder

105ml/7 tbsp mayonnaise

small bunch fresh parsley and dill fronds, to garnish

crispbread, to serve

Per portion Energy 370kcal/1537kJ; Protein 12.7g; Carbohydrate 16.5g, of which sugars 5.2g; Fat 28.5g, of which saturates 4.2g; Cholesterol 178mg; Calcium 45mg; Fibre 1.1g; Sodium 492mg.

Hare pâté
Har pâté

Wild hare are a common sight in Sweden. They are often hunted at the same time as deer and therefore feature in the Swedish diet. The meat is dark, with a sweet flavour and is often compared to venison.

1 Preheat the oven to 140°C/275°F/Gas 1. Butter a 20cm/8in loaf tin (pan) with 15g/½oz of the butter and put 2 bay leaves in the bottom. Melt the remaining butter in a frying pan, add the chicken livers, thyme and remaining bay leaf and, stirring all the time, fry for about 4 minutes until browned. Transfer the livers and their cooking juices to a bowl. Pour over the port and leave to cool.

2 Meanwhile, cut the hare into small cubes. Using a food processor or mincer, mince (grind) half of the meat. Put all the meat in a bowl, add the bacon, cream, eggs, flour, garlic, brandy, nutmeg and pepper and mix together.

3 When the chicken livers have cooled, put the livers and port in a pan and boil until the port has reduced by half to make a sauce. Add the chicken livers and port sauce to the meat mixture and mix together.

4 Put the mixture into the prepared loaf tin and cook in the oven for about 2 hours. Leave to cool in the tin before turning out and serving with toasted brown bread.

Per portion Energy 470kcal/1950kJ; Protein 34.5g; Carbohydrate 3.7g, of which sugars 2.3g; Fat 33g, of which saturates 16.6g; Cholesterol 298mg; Calcium 46mg; Fibre 0.1g; Sodium 1091mg.

Serves 6–8

40g/1½oz/3 tbsp butter

3 bay leaves

250g/9oz chicken livers, trimmed

15ml/1 tbsp fresh thyme

120ml/4fl oz/½ cup port

1 oven-ready hare (jackrabbit)

500g/1¼lb unsmoked bacon, cubed

200ml/7fl oz/scant 1 cup double (heavy) cream

2 eggs

15ml/1 tbsp plain (all-purpose) flour

1 garlic clove, crushed

15ml/1 tbsp brandy

pinch of grated nutmeg

ground black pepper

brown bread, toasted, to serve

Serves 6–8

5 hard-boiled eggs

100g/3½oz can Swedish or matjes anchovies

2 gelatine leaves

200ml/7fl oz/scant 1 cup sour cream

½ red onion, chopped

1 bunch fresh dill, chopped

15ml/1 tbsp Swedish or German mustard

salt and ground black pepper

peeled prawns (shrimp) or lumpfish roe and dill fronds, to garnish

Melba toast or rye bread, to serve

Anchovy terrine
Gubbröra

This dish is based on a traditional Swedish recipe called Old Man's Mix. Just like the English speciality, Gentleman's Relish, it uses anchovies as the main ingredient, in this case the sweet, Swedish variety that are flavoured with cinnamon, cloves and allspice.

1 Line a 20cm/8in terrine with clear film (plastic wrap). Mash the hard-boiled eggs in a bowl. Drain the juice from the anchovy can and add to the eggs. In a large, separate bowl, mash the anchovies.

2 Melt the gelatine as directed on the packet and add to the mashed eggs with the sour cream, mashed anchovies, chopped onion, dill and mustard. Season with salt and pepper to taste and stir thoroughly together. Pour the mixture into the prepared terrine and chill in the refrigerator for 2 hours.

3 To serve, turn out the terrine and garnish with freshly peeled prawns or lumpfish roe and dill fronds. Serve with Melba toast or rye bread.

Per portion Energy 127kcal/529kJ; Protein 8.1g; Carbohydrate 1.8g, of which sugars 1.6g; Fat 9.9g, of which saturates 4.3g; Cholesterol 142mg; Calcium 88mg; Fibre 0.3g; Sodium 602mg.

Cook's tip If you have neither Swedish nor matjes anchovies, soak normal, salted canned anchovies in milk for 2–3 hours before you use them, adding a final sprinkling of ground cinnamon and cloves.

Smoked eel with scrambled eggs
Rökt ål med ägg röra

Smoked eel is a delicacy in Sweden and is often served as part of a buffet on special occasions as well as at other times of the year. The eel is smoked in a special way referred to as "flat smoked eel", and is cut in a similar way to gravlax, sliced thinly at a 45 degree angle. It is smoked without the bone, so it is slightly less gelatinous.

1 Arrange the smoked eel on individual serving plates. Break the eggs into a large bowl and whisk together with the grated nutmeg, cream, salt and pepper.

2 Melt half the butter in a heavy pan over a low heat, add the egg mixture and stir carefully with a wooden spoon until the mixture starts to set. Add the remaining butter and the chopped chives.

3 Serve the eggs immediately with the smoked eel, garnished with a knob of butter to make the scrambled eggs shiny, dill fronds and more black pepper.

Per portion Energy 188kcal/781kJ; Protein 12.1g; Carbohydrate 0.1g, of which sugars 0.1g; Fat 15.7g, of which saturates 6.4g; Cholesterol 291mg; Calcium 44mg; Fibre 0g; Sodium 130mg.

Serves 8

16 slices smoked eel or 8 slices flat smoked eel

10 eggs

a little grated freshly nutmeg

50ml/2fl oz/¼ cup double (heavy) cream

25g/1oz/2 tbsp butter

15ml/1 tbsp chopped fresh chives

salt and ground black pepper

knobs (pats) of butter and dill fronds, to garnish

Västerbotten cheese flan

Västerbotten ost flan

This melt-in-the-mouth light cheese flan is guaranteed to win new fans every time it is served. The flan is easy to make and is delicious when served slightly warm. Swedish Västerbotten is the best cheese to use, but if you cannot get hold of this king of Swedish cheeses, then mature Cheddar cheese is an effective substitute.

1 To prepare the onion marmalade, put the onions in a frying pan with the water, butter and a pinch of salt and simmer for 30 minutes until translucent.

2 Add the sugar to the pan and boil until the mixture has reduced, is golden brown and syrupy in consistency. Finally add the sherry vinegar and reduce again.

3 To make the shortcrust pastry, put the flour and salt in a food processor. Cut the butter and lard or white cooking fat into small pieces, add to the flour then mix together, using a pulsating action, until the mixture resembles fine breadcrumbs. Gradually add the water until the mixture forms a smooth dough. Wrap and store in the refrigerator for 30 minutes or up to 24 hours.

4 Preheat the oven to 200°C/400°F/Gas 6. Roll out the pastry on a lightly floured surface and line a deep 20cm/8in flan tin (pan). Line the pastry with a sheet of greaseproof (waxed) paper and fill with baking beans. Bake blind in the oven for 10–15 minutes until the pastry has set. Remove the flan from the oven and carefully remove the paper and beans then return to the oven for a further 5 minutes until the base is dry.

5 Reduce the oven temperature to 180°C/350°F/Gas 4. Put the cheese, cream, egg yolks and salt and pepper in a bowl and mix them together. Fill the pastry case with the mixture and bake in the oven for 45 minutes until golden brown. Allow to cool and then serve the flan with warm onion marmalade.

Per portion Energy 386kcal/1598kJ; Protein 10.5g; Carbohydrate 14.1g, of which sugars 4.7g; Fat 31.7g, of which saturates 18.5g; Cholesterol 174mg; Calcium 259mg: Fibre 0.9g; Sodium 242mg.

Serves 6–8

90g/3oz/³⁄₄ cup plain (all-purpose) flour

20g/³⁄₄oz/1¹⁄₂ tbsp butter

20g/³⁄₄oz/1¹⁄₂ tbsp lard or white cooking fat

about 15ml/1 tbsp water

225g/¹⁄₂lb Västerbotten or mature (sharp) Cheddar cheese, grated

200ml/7fl oz/³⁄₄ cup double (heavy) cream

4 egg yolks

salt and ground black pepper

For the onion marmalade

300g/11oz onions, finely sliced

100ml/4fl oz/¹⁄₂ cup water

15g/¹⁄₂oz/1 tbsp butter

15ml/1 tbsp sugar

15ml/1 tbsp sherry vinegar

Cook's tips

• Once prepared, the onion marmalade can be stored in a glass jar in the refrigerator for at least two months.

• The flan can also be served with a creamy sauce made with bleak roe (löjrom) or trout roe, mixed with crème fraîche and chopped chives.

Gravlax with mustard and dill sauce
Gravlax med gravlax sås

While this, Sweden's most famous dish, is widely available commercially, home-made gravlax has no comparison. The name, with grav *meaning "hole in the ground" and* lax *meaning "salmon", derives from the fact that it used to be prepared by burying it underground to cure, so that it would remain cool. The key to successful gravlax is the mustard and dill sauce with which it is served.*

Serves 6–8

1kg/2¼lb fresh salmon, filleted and boned, with skin on

50g/2oz/½ cup sea salt

50g/2oz/½ cup caster (superfine) sugar

10ml/2 tsp crushed white peppercorns

200g/7oz/2 cups chopped fresh dill with stalks

fresh dill fronds, to garnish

For the mustard and dill sauce

100g/4oz Swedish mustard

100g/4oz/½ cup sugar

15ml/1 tbsp vinegar

5ml/1 tsp salt

ground black pepper

300ml/½ pint/1¼ cups vegetable oil

100g/4oz/2 cups chopped fresh dill fronds

Cook's tip The mustard and dill sauce can also be served with ham or roast beef. In this case, to give extra piquancy, you can add a tablespoon of HP sauce to the ingredients.

1 Using tweezers, remove any pinbones from the salmon. Then mix the salt and sugar together. Sprinkle a little of the mixture on to the centre of a sheet of foil and place half the salmon fillet, skin side down, on the mixture. Sprinkle the salmon with a little more salt mixture.

2 Sprinkle the white pepper on the flesh side of both salmon fillets and then add the chopped dill to both fillets. Place the second salmon fillet, skin side up, on top of the first fillet and finally sprinkle over the remaining salt mixture.

3 Wrap the foil around the salmon fillets and leave in the refrigerator for 48 hours, turning the salmon every 12 hours. (The foil contains all the juices which help to marinate the salmon.)

4 To make the sauce, put the mustard, sugar, vinegar and salt and pepper into a bowl and mix them all together. Then very slowly drizzle the oil into the mixture, whisking it all the time until you end up with a thick, shiny sauce. Finally add the chopped dill to the mixture.

5 When the salmon has marinated slice it thinly, from one end, at an angle of 45 degrees. Either serve the gravlax on individual serving plates or on one large dish with the dill and mustard sauce. Garnish with dill fronds.

Per portion Energy 543kcal/2258kJ; Protein 26.4g; Carbohydrate 21g, of which sugars 20.7g; Fat 39.8g, of which saturates 5.4g; Cholesterol 63mg; Calcium 58mg; Fibre 0.3g; Sodium 428mg.

Stuffed cabbage rolls
Kåldomar

After Karl XII's invasion of Turkey in 1713 his soldiers brought this dish back to Sweden and replaced the vine leaves with cabbage leaves. Kåldomar are often served as part of the Christmas table in Sweden with a brown sauce. A delicious vegetarian version of the same dish is also given here.

1 Cut the base off the cabbage and separate the leaves. Cook in boiling salted water for 1 minute, drain and remove the hard centre of each leaf.

2 Put the rice and water in a pan, bring to the boil then simmer for 10–12 minutes until the rice is tender. Drain and leave to cool.

3 Preheat the oven to 200°C/400°F/Gas 6. Melt the butter in a pan, add the onion and fry until softened. Put the minced beef in a large bowl and add the onion, cooled rice, beaten egg, thyme, salt and pepper to season.

4 Put 30ml/2 tbsp of the mixture into each leaf and wrap into parcels. Brush the parcels with melted butter and place in an ovenproof dish.

5 Bake for about 40 minutes until golden brown. Serve with boiled new potatoes and lingonberry conserve.

For the vegetarian version

1 Follow step 1 (as above). Put the rice in a pan with a little stock and simmer for 20 minutes, gradually adding the remaining stock and stirring until the rice is tender.

2 Soak the ceps in boiling water. Fry the onion and shallots in 15g/½oz/1 tbsp of the butter until golden brown. Fry the chanterelles or girolles in the remaining butter then drain and add the ceps. Add to the rice with the fried onion, cheese, parsley, salt and pepper.

3 Follow step 4 (as above). Bake at 200°C/400°F/Gas 6 for about 30 minutes until golden brown.

Meat version, per portion Energy 169kcal/702kJ; Protein 9.2g; Carbohydrate 16.1g, of which sugars 5.2g; Fat 7.6g, of which saturates 3.3g; Cholesterol 47mg; Calcium 49mg; Fibre 1.8g; Sodium 51mg.

Vegetarian version, per portion Energy 174kcal/724kJ; Protein 7.1g; Carbohydrate 18.4g, of which sugars 7.1g; Fat 7.8g, of which saturates 4.7g; Cholesterol 20mg; Calcium 157mg; Fibre 3.2g; Sodium 125mg.

Serves 6–8

1 Savoy cabbage

100g/4oz/½ cup long grain rice

100ml/4fl oz/½ cup water

15g/½oz/1 tbsp butter

1 large Spanish (Bermuda) onion, chopped

250g/9oz minced (ground) beef

1 egg, beaten

2.5ml/½ tsp chopped fresh thyme

5ml/1 tsp salt

ground black pepper

melted butter for brushing

boiled new potatoes and lingonberry conserve, to serve

For the vegetarian version

2 pointed cabbages

100g/4oz/½ cup risotto rice

500ml/18fl oz/2½ cups vegetable stock, boiling

50g/2oz dried ceps (porcini mushrooms)

1 Spanish (Bermuda) onion, chopped

2 shallots, chopped

30g/1oz/2 tbsp butter

400g/14oz chanterelle or girolle mushrooms

100g/4oz mature (sharp) Cheddar or Västerbotten cheese, grated

20g/¾oz chopped fresh parsley

salt and ground black pepper

melted butter for brushing

lingonberry conserve, to serve

Fish &
shellfish

Poached turbot with
   egg and prawns

Jansson's temptation

Poached cod with parsnips

Smoked pike with crème
   fraîche and chives

Fried mackerel with
   rhubarb chutney

Dillflower crayfish

Crab gratin

Lax pudding

Sautéed perch with girolles

Salted salmon with potatoes in
   dill sauce

Fried mustard herrings
   with mangetouts

Mackerel, crayfish
and fruity sauces

Fish, whether fresh, smoked or pickled, has always been a staple food for the Swedes. Since Sweden is surrounded by water and has a myriad of lakes and streams, there is an abundance of sea and freshwater fish available. The most commonly eaten freshwater fish is salmon, which swims in the rivers as well as being farmed. Salmon is commonly eaten in both its fresh and smoked varieties, the latter given here in the tasty winter-warmer recipe for Lax Pudding. Another of the nation's favourite fish is herring, and the rich combination of flavours in the recipe for Fried Mustard Herrings is addictively mouthwatering, along with one of Sweden's best-known dishes, Jansson's Temptation, a satisfying gratin of canned and fresh anchovies or sprats combined with potatoes and onions.

On the west coast of Sweden, crab is plentiful and inexpensive. Freshwater crayfish, too, are popular, and are often cooked in dill-flavoured water, as given in the Dillflower Crayfish recipe included here. There is also a popular local prawn (shrimp) called "räkor", found in the North Sea round Gothenburg, which are distinctive for their long front whiskers. However, any fresh prawns can be used, preferably large ones which usually indicate a better quality.

Serves 6–8

1kg/2¼lb whole turbot, gutted

1 leek, finely chopped

1 bunch fresh parsley, chopped

1 lemon, sliced

salt and ground black pepper

For the sauce

250g/9oz/1 cup plus 2 tbsp butter

1 egg

175g/6oz shell-on cooked prawns
(shrimp)

15ml/1 tbsp grated fresh horseradish

Poached turbot with egg and prawns
Kokt piggvar med ägg, räk och pepparot sås

*Turbot, known as the king of flat fish because of its firm, white flesh and
delicate flavour, is found mostly in the North Sea on the west coast of Sweden.
This fish is also caught in the south-west of the Baltic Sea, where freshwater
fish are found in salt water. In Sweden, turbot is often irreverently called "dass
lock", meaning toilet seat, which is a reference to its expansive flat shape.
If unavailable, halibut, sole or flounder are good substitutes.*

1 Preheat the oven to 180°C/350°F/Gas 4. Lay the gutted turbot on a large
sheet of foil.

2 Mix together the chopped leek and parsley and season with salt and pepper.

3 Use the leek and parsley mixture to stuff the body cavity of the turbot and
then add the lemon slices. Wrap the turbot in the foil and bake the fish in the
oven for 45 minutes.

4 To make the sauce, hard boil the egg and leave to cool. Then mash the hard-
boiled egg in a bowl.

5 Melt the butter and set aside. Remove the shells from the prawns and add them
to the mashed hard-boiled egg with the butter and grated horseradish.

6 Serve the turbot on a large serving dish, accompanied by the sauce.

Per portion Energy 350kcal/1448kJ; Protein 20.8g; Carbohydrate 0.8g, of which sugars 0.7g; Fat 29.2g,
of which saturates 17.1g; Cholesterol 113mg; Calcium 71mg; Fibre 0.5g; Sodium 337mg.

Jansson's temptation
Jansson's frestelse

This anchovy pie is another warming dish for the winter months. The dish is named after a well-known Swedish opera singer whose name was Jansson, who served it to his guests after a performance at the opera house in Stockholm. In Sweden, a meal such as this, called "vickning", is served late in the evening at the end of a good party, and is always accompanied by snaps. It is also excellent served as part of a smörgåsbord selection.

1 Preheat the oven to 180°C/350°F/Gas 4. Peel and grate the potatoes. Put in a sieve (strainer) and wash under cold running water to remove any excess starch. Drain well and put in a bowl. Add the sliced onion and mix together then put in a shallow, ovenproof dish.

2 Mix together the milk and cream. Put both the liquid and the fish from the can of anchovies into the milk mixture and stir together. Pour the mixture over the potatoes and season with salt and pepper. Bake in the oven for 50 minutes until golden brown and bubbling.

Per portion Energy 400kcal/1669kJ; Protein 9.4g; Carbohydrate 36.5g, of which sugars 6.1g; Fat 25.1g, of which saturates 14.6g; Cholesterol 69mg; Calcium 115mg; Fibre 2.5g; Sodium 696mg.

Serves 6

6 large potatoes

1 Spanish (Bermuda) onion, thinly sliced

120ml/4fl oz/½ cup milk

250ml/8fl oz/1 cup double (heavy) cream

100g/3½oz can Swedish anchovies

salt and ground black pepper

Cook's tips
• This dish is delicious served on its own or with a salad and is also perfect when eaten with cold sliced ham.
• If you cannot get Swedish anchovies, use ordinary salted anchovies and soak them in milk for a couple of hours to remove the saltiness.

Serves 6

6 cod steaks, with skin on, about 150g/5oz each

30ml/2 tbsp sea salt

6 small carrots, sliced lengthways into quarters

3 parsnips, sliced lengthways into quarters

10g/⅓oz/1 tsp sugar

115g/4oz/½ cup butter

30ml/2 tbsp grated fresh horseradish

salt and ground white pepper

fresh parsley, chopped, to garnish

Cook's tip This dish can also be made with pike or sea bass. If you use sea bass, it is advisable to cook it whole rather than in steaks.

Poached cod with parsnips
Pocherad torsk med palsternacka

The Swedish fishing industry heavily relies on catching cod, which is second only to herring in terms of numbers fished. Cod and carrots are an almost sacred combination in Sweden, but this recipe rings some changes by adding parsnips.

1 Cover the cod pieces in the salt and put in the refrigerator for 2–3 hours. (This salting process will help to firm the flesh and give it a mother-of-pearl shimmer.)

2 Put the carrots and parsnips in a pan. Add the sugar, a knob (pat) of the butter and salt and pepper and pour in enough water to cover the vegetables. Cut a piece of greaseproof (waxed) paper to fit the inside of the pan and place on top of the vegetables. (This allows the vegetables to cook in their own juice.) Simmer the vegetables, without a lid, for about 10 minutes until the water has evaporated.

3 Put the cod steaks on to an upside-down plate, sitting in the base of a pan, and pour a little water into the pan. Cover and steam the fish for about 8–10 minutes until just tender, without overcooking the fish. (This traditional method is an effective way to steam fish because it doesn't lose its flavour and won't dry out.)

4 To make the horseradish sauce, melt the remaining butter and then add the grated horseradish. Serve the cod steaks garnished with parsley and accompany with the sauce and vegetables.

Per portion Energy 321kcal/1336kJ; Protein 28.8g; Carbohydrate 11.6g, of which sugars 7.9g; Fat 17.9g, of which saturates 10.3g; Cholesterol 111mg; Calcium 49mg; Fibre 3.2g; Sodium 265mg.

Smoked pike with crème fraîche and chives
Rökt gädda med gräddfil och gräslök

Sweden is a land of forests and lakes, home to a wealth of natural produce. This recipe was inspired by a sailing trip to the Stockholm archipelago where a freshly caught pike was wrapped in wet newspapers and cooked on a small bonfire. This method of preparing fish is unexpectedly delicious and satisfyingly simple. If it's not convenient to make a bonfire, the dish can also be prepared on a garden barbecue.

1 Sprinkle the salt all over the pike or eel and leave for about 1 hour. Put the juniper berries, thyme and olive oil in a mortar and pestle and grind together. Add the chopped onion and mix together.

2 Use the herb mixture and quartered lemon to stuff the body cavity of the pike or eel. Hold about five layers of newspaper under cold running water so that it becomes completely wet (it needs to be saturated otherwise the fish will burn) and then use it to wrap around the pike or eel.

3 Put the parcel on top of a smouldering bonfire, either placed on a grill (broiler) rack or on top of damp leaves placed over burning logs, and leave to smoke for 25–30 minutes until cooked. Alternatively, cook the fish on a barbecue. Take the fish off the fire, unwrap the newspaper and sprinkle with chopped chives to garnish. Serve with spoonfuls of crème fraîche.

Per portion Energy 195kcal/818kJ; Protein 28.5g; Carbohydrate 0.8g, of which sugars 0.6g; Fat 8.7g, of which saturates 0.2g; Cholesterol 0mg; Calcium 124mg; Fibre 0.4g; Sodium 80mg.

Serves 6–8

300g/11oz/3 cups sea salt

2kg/4½lb pike or eel, gutted

15ml/1 tbsp juniper berries

2–3 sprigs fresh thyme

15ml/1 tbsp olive oil

1 red onion, finely chopped

1 lemon, quartered

newspaper

chopped fresh chives, to garnish

crème fraîche, to serve

Cook's tip
To cook the fish more quickly, turn the newspaper package on the bonfire or barbecue every 2–3 minutes and continue to wet down the paper. The fish will then take about 15 minutes.

Serves 6

6 mackerel fillets, skinned

60ml/4 tbsp plain (all-purpose) white flour

30ml/2 tbsp vegetable oil

25g/1oz/2 tbsp butter

salt and ground black pepper

boiled new potatoes, to serve

For the rhubarb chutney

150g/5oz fresh rhubarb

50g/2oz/¼ cup caster (superfine) sugar

5ml/1 tsp cider vinegar

a knob (pat) of butter

Cook's tip Replace the rhubarb in the chutney recipe with gooseberries to make gooseberry chutney instead.

Fried mackerel with rhubarb chutney
Makril med rabarber chutney

Mackerel is an undervalued and inexpensive fish. It has a wonderful flavour and, as an oily fish, is very good for you. Because of its oiliness and distinctive flavour it is best served with something tart such as a squeeze of lemon or, as in this recipe, rhubarb.

1 To make the rhubarb chutney, cut the rhubarb into small pieces and put in a pan with the sugar and vinegar. Simmer for about 6 minutes until soft but not mushy. Stir in the butter.

2 Dust the mackerel with the flour and season with salt and pepper. Heat the oil and butter in a large frying pan, add the mackerel fillets and fry for 2–3 minutes on each side until golden brown.

3 Warm the chutney in the pan. Serve the mackerel with the rhubarb chutney and new potatoes.

Per portion Energy 353kcal/1470kJ; Protein 19.9g; Carbohydrate 16.7g, of which sugars 9.1g; Fat 23.4g, of which saturates 5.9g; Cholesterol 63mg; Calcium 54mg; Fibre 0.7g; Sodium 90mg.

Dillflower crayfish
Kräftor med krondill

Eating crayfish in August and September is almost a sacred ritual in Sweden and Finland. For years it was possible to eat local crayfish but they are now almost extinct and have been replaced by a hardy American type called the Signal crayfish. This dish is eaten as a celebration, at which snaps and beer are served and amusing songs are sung.

Serves 6–8

2kg/4½lb live freshwater crayfish

3 litres/5 pints/12 cups water

100g/4oz/1 cup coarse sea salt

2 sugar lumps

1 onion, chopped

350ml/12fl oz bottle stout

1 large bunch dill flowers (available from florists in the summer season or use dill seeds to infuse the crayfish with a similar flavour)

Västerbotten or mature (sharp) Cheddar cheese and toasted bread, to serve

1 Put the crayfish in strong plastic bags, about 10–15 per bag, seal and place in the freezer for 2 hours to put them to sleep. (This is the most humane and least traumatic way of killing them.) Many people, however, are convinced that crayfish taste far superior when they are cooked fresh, in which case they should be added live at step 3.

2 Put the water, salt and sugar in a large pan and bring to the boil. Meanwhile, put the dill flowers in a large bowl, reserving a few flowers to garnish, and add the chopped onion and stout.

3 Remove a bag of crayfish from the freezer, unseal the bag and immediately drop the unconscious crayfish into the boiling water. Cover the pan, return to the boil and cook for about 8 minutes, until the crayfish turn a bright orange colour. Using a slotted spoon, remove the crayfish from the water and place on top of the dill flowers. Repeat with the remaining crayfish until they are all cooked.

4 Pour the hot cooking liquid over the crayfish and allow to cool in the liquid then leave to marinate in the refrigerator overnight. The strong flavour of the dill flowers will infuse the crayfish.

5 Serve the crayfish the following day, garnished with the reserved fresh dill flowers and accompanied with cheese and toast. Serve with snaps and beer!

Cook's tip The best way to eat crayfish is with a crayfish knife, a sharp pointed knife that always has a red handle. However, many people simply break the shell with their teeth and then suck out the juice.

Per portion Energy 115kcal/481kJ; Protein 21.7g; Carbohydrate 1.1g, of which sugars 0.9g; Fat 1.8g, of which saturates 0.5g; Cholesterol 78mg; Calcium 141mg; Fibre 0.1g; Sodium 1527mg.

Crab gratin
Gratinerad krabba

Crab is prolific on the west coast of Sweden. This dish is a filling main course and a remnant of an older era, but such traditional comfort food still holds pride of place in many kitchens. This recipe is definitely one to impress your friends. The dish can also be made using around 18 langoustines instead of the crab. In this case, cook them for about 10 minutes, until they turn a bright orange.

1 Put the crabs in individual, strong plastic bags, seal and place in the freezer for 2 hours to put them to sleep (this is the most humane and least traumatizing way of killing them).

2 Put the water, beer, salt and sugar in a very large pan and bring to the boil. Remove 1–2 crabs, depending upon the size of your pan, from the freezer, unseal the bag and immediately drop the unconscious crabs into the boiling water. Cover the pan, return to the boil and cook for 15 minutes, allowing an extra 10 minutes for each additional crab. Then remove the cooked crab from the water and transfer to a large bowl. Repeat with the remaining crabs until they are all cooked.

3 Pour the hot cooking liquid over the crabs, allow to cool in the liquid and then leave in the refrigerator overnight.

4 Remove the crabs from the liquid and reserve 300ml/½ pint/1¼ cups. Put the crab on a chopping board on its back to extract the meat. Hold a claw firmly in one hand and twist to remove it. Remove the remaining claw and legs in the same way. Break the claws in half by bending them backwards then crack the shells with a nutcracker or rolling pin and hook out the meat with a skewer. Remove the stomach sac and mouth and discard. Hold the shell firmly and press the body section upwards and gently pull them apart. Remove the grey gills and discard then cut the body into small pieces and hook out the meat. Finally, scoop the brown meat out of the shell.

5 Preheat the oven to 200°C/400°F/Gas 6. To make the sauce, melt the butter in a pan, add the flour and cook over a low heat for 1 minute, stirring to make a roux. Remove from the heat and slowly add the reserved liquid, stirring all the time, to form a smooth sauce. Return to the heat and cook, stirring, for 2–3 minutes until the sauce boils and thickens. Remove from the heat, stir in the cream then add the egg yolks and brandy anchovy liquid and season to taste with salt and pepper.

5 Add the extracted crab meat to the sauce and then put the mixture into the empty crab shells. Then sprinkle the grated Cheddar cheese on top and bake in the oven for 10–15 minutes until the crab meat mixture is golden brown. Serve hot, with boiled rice.

Per portion Energy 544kcal/2244kJ; Protein 10.9g; Carbohydrate 6.1g, of which sugars 4.2g; Fat 51.7g, of which saturates 30.8g; Cholesterol 209mg; Calcium 112mg; Fibre 0.1g; Sodium 216mg.

Serves 6

6 large crabs

3 litres/2½ pints/6¼ cups water

350ml/12fl oz beer

100g/4oz/1 cup coarse sea salt

2 sugar lumps

40g/1½oz Cheddar cheese, grated

boiled basmati rice, to serve

For the sauce

25g/1oz/2 tbsp butter

15ml/1 tbsp plain (all-purpose) flour

475ml/16fl oz/2 cups double (heavy) cream

2 egg yolks

30ml/2 tbsp brandy

10ml/2 tsp liquid from a can of Swedish anchovies, or other fish stock

salt and ground black pepper

Cook's tip Instead of boiling the live crabs yourself, you could use 500g/1¼lb fresh crabmeat, thawed if frozen. You will then also need 300ml/½ pint/1¼ cups fish stock to make the sauce.

Lax pudding
Lax pudding

This mouthwatering winter warmer – a classic dish from the Swedish husmanskost, or home cooking – is an excellent way to use up any remaining smoked salmon or gravlax.This is a good alternative to fish pie, with similar ingredients, but a quite different preparation method. The dill is what makes Lax Pudding so essentially Swedish.

1 Cook the potatoes in boiling salted water for 15–20 minutes until tender. Drain and leave to cool. Meanwhile, melt the butter in a pan. Add the sliced leek and sauté gently until softened.

2 Preheat the oven to 180°C/350°F/Gas 4. Thinly slice the cooled potatoes and place in a layer in the bottom of a terrine. Add 1–3 slices of gravlax and then add a layer of leeks. Repeat these layers, using all the ingredients, finishing with a neat layer of potatoes. Sprinkle over the chopped dill.

3 Beat the eggs in a jug (pitcher) or bowl. Add the milk and cream and beat together then season with salt and pepper. Pour the egg mixture into the terrine. Bake in the oven for about 30 minutes until golden brown.

Per portion Energy 137kcal/573kJ; Protein 9.9g; Carbohydrate 7.2g, of which sugars 2.4g; Fat 7.8g, of which saturates 3.9g; Cholesterol 70mg; Calcium 59mg; Fibre 0.8g; Sodium 525mg.

Serves 8

250g/9oz new potatoes

25g/1oz/2 tbsp butter

1 leek, sliced

200g/7oz gravlax, about 8 slices

a little chopped fresh dill

2 eggs

250ml/8fl oz/1 cup milk

30ml/2 tbsp double (heavy) cream

salt and ground black pepper

Cook's tip The terrine can be finished with a garnish of 25g/1oz melted butter to which 30ml/2 tbsp chopped fresh parsley has been added.

Serves 6

300g/11oz girolle or chanterelle mushrooms

50g/2oz/¼ cup butter

1 onion, chopped

75g/3oz/⅔ cup plain (all-purpose) flour

6 perch, about 500g/1¼lb, scaled and filleted (cod is a good alternative)

1 bunch fresh parsley, about 25g/1oz, finely chopped

salt and ground black pepper

boiled new potatoes, to serve

Cook's tips

• Perch have a spiky fin, so take care in the initial stages of preparation.

• You can ask your fishmonger to scale and fillet the fish, but if you need to scale the perch yourself do so with a knife, and work in a bowl of water so that the scales don't go everywhere.

• To fillet the fish, cut along the backbone from head to tail to expose the backbone. Then, with smooth cutting strokes, separate the flesh from the bones. Turn the fish over and repeat on the other side.

Sautéed perch with girolles
Stekt abborre med kantareller

Perch and girolle mushrooms are a classic combination because the earthy taste of the perch complements the apricot perfume of the mushrooms. The best time to catch perch is in the autumn and this is also when girolles are in season. Don't remove the skin because that is where most of their delicious flavour is.

1 Slice the mushrooms if large, otherwise leave them whole. Melt 25g/1oz/2 tbsp of the butter in a large frying pan, add the mushrooms and onion and fry until golden.

2 Season the flour with salt and pepper and use to dust the fish fillets. In a separate large frying pan, melt the remaining butter, add the fish fillets and fry over a medium heat for 2–3 minutes on each side.

3 Add the chopped parsley to the mushroom and onion mixture and serve with the perch. Accompany with boiled new potatoes.

Per portion Energy 181kcal/760kJ; Protein 17.5g; Carbohydrate 10.8g, of which sugars 0.9g; Fat 7.9g, of which saturates 4.5g; Cholesterol 56mg; Calcium 32mg; Fibre 1.1g; Sodium 104mg.

Serves 6–8

200g/7oz/2 cups sea salt

50g/2oz/½ cup caster (superfine) sugar

1kg/2¼lb salmon, scaled, filleted and boned

1 litre/1¾ pints/4 cups water

675–900g/1½–2lb new potatoes

For the béchamel and dill sauce

25g/1oz/2 tbsp butter

45ml/3 tbsp plain (all-purpose) flour

750ml/1¼ pints/3 cups milk

120ml/4fl oz/½ cup double (heavy) cream

a little freshly grated nutmeg (optional)

25g/1oz/¼ cup chopped fresh dill

salt and ground black pepper

Salted salmon with potatoes in dill sauce
Rimmad lax med dillstuvad potatis

Rimmad lax or salted salmon is a refreshing alternative to the more commonly known gravlax recipe. Personally, I prefer rimmad lax, because it is plumper, smoother and fresher. This dish is delicious with creamy potatoes and dill, which counteracts the saltiness of the fish.

1 Mix together 100g/4oz/1 cup of the salt and the sugar. Cover the salmon fillets with the mixture and put in a plastic bag. Seal the bag and put the fish on a plate in the refrigerator overnight.

2 The next day, make a brine by mixing the remaining salt and the water in a bowl. Place the salmon in the brine and leave in the refrigerator for another night.

3 Remove the salmon from the brine and cut into 5mm/¼in slices. If large, cut the potatoes in half then cook in boiling water for about 20 minutes until tender.

4 Meanwhile, make the béchamel sauce. Melt the butter in a pan, add the flour and cook over a low heat for 1 minute, stirring to make a roux. Remove from the heat and slowly add the milk, stirring all the time, to form a smooth sauce. Return to the heat and cook, stirring, for 2–3 minutes until the sauce boils and thickens. Stir in the cream, nutmeg if using, salt and pepper to taste and heat gently.

5 Drain the cooked potatoes and add to the sauce with the chopped dill. Serve the salted salmon with the potatoes in béchamel and dill.

Per portion Energy 407kcal/1699kJ; Protein 26.4g; Carbohydrate 22.6g, of which sugars 5.9g; Fat 24g, of which saturates 9.7g; Cholesterol 85mg; Calcium 155mg; Fibre 1g; Sodium 118mg.

Fried mustard herrings with mangetouts
Stekt senap sill med socker ärtor

Because of the Swedish mustard and dill that are used in the gravlax sauce this dish has a classic Swedish character. The herrings have to be fresh as they lose their delicious flavour if they are kept for too long. The mangetouts can be replaced with sugar snap peas.

1 To make the sauce, put the mustard, sugar, vinegar, salt and pepper to season into a bowl, mix together then very slowly drizzle the oil into the mixture, whisking it all the time until you have a thick, shiny sauce. Add the chopped dill.

2 If necessary, remove any fins or scales from the herring fillets then rinse under cold running water and dry on kitchen paper. Cut the fillets in half lengthways then add to the bowl of sauce. Place in the refrigerator overnight to marinate.

3 Put the breadcrumbs and flour on a large plate and season with salt and pepper. Coat the fish fillets, on both sides, in the mixture. Heat the butter and oil in a large frying pan, add the herring fillets and fry on both sides until golden brown.

4 Meanwhile, put the mangetouts in a steamer and cook for 5 minutes. Serve the herrings with the mangetouts and mashed potatoes.

Per portion Energy 730kcal/3032kJ; Protein 25.1g; Carbohydrate 30.7g, of which sugars 4.5g; Fat 57.2g, of which saturates 11.9g; Cholesterol 68mg; Calcium 152mg; Fibre 2.7g; Sodium 728mg.

Serves 6

6 fresh herrings, filleted

50g/2oz/1 cup fresh breadcrumbs

150g/5oz/1¼ cups plain (all-purpose) flour

50g/2oz/¼ cup butter

15ml/1 tbsp vegetable oil

450g/1lb mangetouts (snow peas)

salt and ground black pepper

mashed potatoes, to serve

For the mustard and dill sauce

100g/4oz Swedish mustard

100g/4oz/½ cup sugar

15ml/1 tbsp cider vinegar

5ml/1 tsp salt

ground black pepper

300ml/½ pint/1¼ cups vegetable oil

100g/4oz chopped fresh dill fronds

Domestic
meat

Lamb stew in a
creamy dill sauce

Gotland lamb burgers stuffed
with blue cheese

Beef à la Lindström

Swedish hash

Beef Rydberg

Sailor's steak

Stuffed loin of pork with prunes
and hasselback potatoes

Braised pig's cheeks with
mashed swedes

Christmas ham with Swedish
mustard

Baked sausage terrine with
lingonberry conserve

Calf's liver with bacon and
capers

Sweetbreads with pancetta

Swedish hash
and crispy crust pork

Sweden is well known for its organic farming methods and, as a result, its domestic meat is full of flavour. Gotland, a small island off the south-east coast of Sweden, has an extensive undeveloped landscape that makes it suitable for farming a high volume of organic meat and it produces the most delicious lamb. The recipe for Lamb Burgers Stuffed with Blue Cheese has its roots in Gotland – the region also produces a distinctive blue cheese which is traditionally used in this recipe.

Cows in Sweden are reared under the same exemplary farming standards, whether a beef or a dairy herd. In the kitchen, beef is often combined with ingredients that have an interesting bite, such as Beef à la Lindström with beetroot and capers and Sailor's Steak where the beef is cooked in ale. Pork is a popular main ingredient for meals and it is a well-established tradition to eat ham for supper on Christmas Eve, in combination with Swedish mustard.

Well-known Swedish meat dishes and the most common home-cooked dishes include Swedish Meatballs, the national dish that can be prepared with a combination of beef and pork, or elk (see Elk Meatballs with Lingon in the Wild Meat chapter), and the popular dish Pytt-i-panna, or Swedish Hash.

Serves 6–8

1kg/2¼lb lamb neck fillet or boned leg, cubed

1 Spanish (Bermuda) onion, roughly chopped

1 carrot, chopped

1 celery stick, chopped

1 bay leaf

2 sprigs fresh thyme

For the sauce

1 bunch fresh dill

250ml/8fl oz/1 cup water

90g/3½oz/½ cup sugar

120ml/4fl oz/½ cup white vinegar

10g/¼oz/½ tbsp butter, softened

10g/¼oz/½ tbsp plain (all-purpose) flour

1 egg yolk

120ml/4fl oz/½ cup double (heavy) cream

salt and ground black pepper

Cook's tip The ideal accompaniment for the lamb stew is boiled new potatoes drizzled with butter.

Lamb stew in a creamy dill sauce
Dillkött

The Baltic island of Gotland, off the south-east coast of Sweden, has many herds of sheep which thrive in its extensive landscape and the island is well known for its lamb production. This dish is strongly associated with the region, but is popular in the south, too, where lamb is also farmed.

1 Put the cubed lamb in a large pan and then add the onion, carrot, celery, bay leaf and thyme. Pour in enough cold water to cover the ingredients fully, bring to simmering point and then simmer for about 40 minutes to 1 hour until the meat is tender.

2 To make the sauce, remove the dill fronds from the main stalks, reserving the stalks, chop finely and set aside. Put the reserved stalks in a pan and add the water, sugar and vinegar. Bring to the boil then boil for 5 minutes.

3 Meanwhile, put the butter in a bowl and work in the flour with a fork until smooth to make a beurre manié. Mix the egg yolk and cream together.

4 When the lamb is cooked, put 1 litre/1¾ pints/4 cups of the stock from the lamb in a pan. Strain in the sugar and vinegar liquid then bring the mixture to simmering point. Add small knobs (pats) of the beurre manié, whisking vigorously, and allow each knob to melt before adding another, to thicken the sauce. Bring to the boil then simmer for about 10 minutes.

5 Stir the egg and cream mixture and the chopped dill fronds into the sauce. Do not allow the mixture to boil or the sauce will curdle.

6 Pour the sauce over the lamb to serve.

Per portion Energy 509kcal/2125kJ; Protein 34.4g; Carbohydrate 22.6g, of which sugars 20.1g; Fat 31.8g, of which saturates 16g; Cholesterol 191mg; Calcium 56mg; Fibre 1.2g; Sodium 169mg.

Gotland lamb burgers stuffed with blue cheese
Lamburgare från Gotland med ädelost

Lamb burgers are much healthier than beef burgers because they contain far less saturated fat. The lamb adds a gamey, rich quality to these burgers, a dish originating from the island of Gotland, and the blue cheese and crème fraîche give them a creamy consistency.

1 Peel the potatoes, cut into quarters and cook in boiling water for about 20 minutes until tender. When the potatoes are cooked, drain, return to the pan and mash well. Heat the milk with 25g/1oz/2 tbsp of the butter and beat them well into the potato mash.

2 Put the mashed potatoes in a large bowl. Add the egg, chopped onion, crème fraîche, mustard seeds, salt and pepper and mix well together. Add the minced lamb and mix again.

3 Form the mixture into 16 even-size, round, flat burgers. Spoon a little of the blue cheese on the centre of 8 of the burgers and then place the remaining burgers on top to make 8 larger burgers.

4 Melt the remaining butter in a large frying pan. Add the burgers and fry for 3 minutes on each side, until golden brown and the cheese has melted. Serve hot.

Per portion Energy 345kcal/1433kJ; Protein 18g; Carbohydrate 7g, of which sugars 1.2g; Fat 27.2g, of which saturates 16.5g; Cholesterol 116mg; Calcium 116mg; Fibre 0.5g; Sodium 310mg.

Serves 8

2 potatoes

60ml/4 fl oz/½ cup milk

50g/2oz/4 tbsp butter

1 egg, beaten

1 red onion, chopped

100ml/4fl oz/½ cup crème fraîche

15ml/1 tbsp mustard seeds

400g/14oz minced (ground) lamb

225g/8oz/1 cup blue cheese such as Gorgonzola or Stilton

salt and ground black pepper

Cook's tips The burgers can be made with minced (ground) venison. They are also good served with mashed potatoes and leeks sliced and lightly fried in butter.

Serves 6–8

800g/1¾lb minced (ground) beef

3 egg yolks

250g/9oz onion, finely chopped

130g/4½oz cooked beetroot (beet), finely chopped

175g/6oz/1 cup capers

a knob (pat) of butter

15ml/1 tbsp vegetable oil

salt and ground black pepper

Cook's tip The burgers are delicious served with mashed or fried cubed potatoes and seasonal vegetables, and a glass of cold beer.

Beef à la Lindström
Biff à la Lindström

This dish, resembling a hamburger, is named after Henrik Lindström, a Swedish industrialist who spent much of his time in Russia in the mid-19th century. He often ate at the Hotel Witt in the city of Kalmar in the south-east of Sweden where he used to ask the head chef to prepare his minced steak the Russian way by adding capers and beetroot. This recipe has, ever since, been a Swedish favourite.

1 Put the beef, egg yolks, onion, beetroot and capers in a bowl. Season with salt and pepper and mix together. Form the mixture into even-size round, flat burgers.

2 Heat the butter and oil in a large frying pan. Add the burgers and fry, turning them once, until browned on both sides but still slightly pink in the centre. Serve hot.

Per portion Energy 282kcal/1169kJ; Protein 21.7g; Carbohydrate 4.3g, of which sugars 3.5g; Fat 19.8g, of which saturates 7.7g; Cholesterol 137mg; Calcium 34mg; Fibre 0.9g; Sodium 103mg.

Swedish hash
Pytt-i-panna

A classic Swedish dish, Pytt-i-panna literally means "put in the pan". Originally introduced as an economy dish made with leftovers, its popularity has meant that it is invariably now made from fresh ingredients. Similar in many ways to the Biff Rydberg recipe (see page 70), both recipes use frankfurter sausages to give a little piquancy. In this recipe all the ingredients are mixed together by the cook, whereas in Biff Rydberg, the ingredients are served separately and it is the diner who mixes the ingredients together.

1 Peel and cut the potatoes into small cubes measuring about 3mm/⅛in. Heat the butter and oil in a large frying pan, add the potato cubes and fry for about 20 minutes, stirring frequently, until golden brown. Remove from the pan with a slotted spoon, put in a bowl and keep warm.

2 Put the onion in the pan, adding more butter if necessary, and fry until golden brown. Remove from the pan and add to the potatoes. Add the gammon or bacon and the frankfurter sausages, fry until cooked and put them in the bowl.

3 Fry the beef or lamb until heated through and add to the other fried ingredients. Season the mixture with salt and pepper to taste and mix together.

4 Serve the mixture on warmed, individual serving plates. Break the eggs, one at a time, separating the yolks from the whites, and putting an egg yolk in half its shell in the centre of each plate. Garnish with chopped parsley and serve with Worcestershire sauce.

Serves 3–4

4 large potatoes

about 25g/1oz/2 tbsp butter

15ml/1 tbsp vegetable oil

1 large onion, finely chopped

150g/5oz gammon (smoked or cured ham) or bacon, finely chopped

100g/4oz smoked frankfurters, finely chopped

500g/1¼lb cold cooked lamb or beef, cubed

salt and ground black pepper

3–4 very fresh eggs, to serve

Worcestershire sauce, to serve

chopped fresh parsley, to garnish

Cook's tips
• 1–2 tablespoons of capers can be included in the mixture. Add them to the pan with the meat.
• Make sure that the eggs are fresh and, because the recipe contains raw egg yolks, do not serve the dish to infants, the elderly, pregnant women, and convalescents.
• The dish can also be served with fried eggs and beetroot (beet) or sour pickled gherkin.

Per portion Energy 930kcal/3866kJ; Protein 55.9g; Carbohydrate 18.7g, of which sugars 3.6g; Fat 70.9g, of which saturates 28.8g; Cholesterol 427mg; Calcium 68mg; Fibre 1.3g; Sodium 1992mg.

Beef Rydberg
Biff Rydberg

The Hotel Rydberg, which overlooked the Royal Palace in Stockholm, closed in 1914 but is still remembered for this recipe that was popularly served there at the turn of the century. Using fillet steak (instead of the original kidneys) and potatoes, it is a luxury version of the classic Swedish hash Pytt-i-panna.

1 Peel and cut the potatoes into small cubes measuring about 3mm/⅛in. Cut the steak and onions into cubes the same size as the potatoes.

2 Heat the butter and oil in a frying pan, add the onions and fry until golden brown. Using a slotted spoon, remove from the pan. Add the potatoes, adding more butter if necessary, and fry for about 20 minutes until golden brown. Remove from the pan.

3 Just before serving, so that the steak is not overcooked, add the steak cubes to the pan and fry for less than a minute, until sealed but still rare.

4 Arrange small piles of the fried steak cubes, the fried potatoes and the fried onions on individual serving plates. Break the eggs, one at a time, separating the yolks from the whites, and putting the egg yolks in half the shell in the middle of the plates.

5 Serve at once with brown sauce, Worcestershire sauce, mustard and tomato ketchup so that each person can season the dish according to their taste. Diners should then mix all the ingredients together and combine them with the raw egg yolk.

Per portion Energy 407kcal/1711kJ; Protein 26.4g; Carbohydrate 46.9g, of which sugars 6.3g; Fat 13.9g, of which saturates 7.4g; Cholesterol 79mg; Calcium 34mg; Fibre 3.4g; Sodium 125mg.

Serves 6

8 large potatoes

600g/1lb 6oz fillet steak

2 onions

about 50g/2oz/¼ cup butter

15ml/1 tbsp vegetable oil

salt and ground black pepper

6 very fresh eggs, to serve

Brown sauce, Worcestershire sauce, mustard and tomato ketchup, to serve

Cook's tip Because of the raw egg yolk, this dish should not be served to young children, the elderly, pregnant women or convalescents and anyone suffering from an illness. It is essential that the eggs used are very fresh.

Sailor's steak
Sjöman's biff

Also known as seaman's beef, this dish used to be associated with sailors because it requires very few kitchen utensils and just one pot to make it. Cooking the meat and vegetables together gives the dish a delicious stew-like combination of textures and flavours.

1 Preheat the oven to 180°C/350°F/Gas 4. Using a rolling pin or heavy wooden mallet, beat the steaks until flattened. Peel the potatoes, cut in half and then into 1cm/$\frac{1}{2}$in slices.

2 Melt the butter in a large flameproof casserole. Add the onions and fry for about 10 minutes until golden brown. Push the onions to one side of the dish, add the steaks and fry until sealed on both sides. Add the sliced potatoes, thyme, bay leaves, salt and pepper.

3 Pour the ale over the ingredients in the dish, cover with a lid and bake in the oven for about 1 hour until the potatoes are tender. Sprinkle chopped parsley on top to garnish and serve with pickled beetroot or pickled gherkins.

Per portion Energy 279kcal/1170kJ; Protein 19.4g; Carbohydrate 29.9g, of which sugars 9.7g; Fat 6.6g, of which saturates 3.2g; Cholesterol 50mg; Calcium 38mg; Fibre 2.3g; Sodium 70mg.

Serves 8

8 thin slices entrecôte (sirloin) steak, about 600g/1lb 6oz

8 medium potatoes

15g/$\frac{1}{2}$oz/1 tbsp butter

4 onions, chopped

1 sprig fresh thyme

2 bay leaves

500ml/17fl oz bottle ale

salt and ground black pepper

15ml/1 tbsp chopped fresh parsley, to garnish

pickled beetroot (beet) or pickled gherkins, to serve

Stuffed loin of pork with prunes and hasselback potatoes

Rostad fläsk stek med plommon

The Swedes love the taste of pork and this recipe is a real favourite. Here, the roast pork is served with hasselback potatoes, which are the Swedish version of roast potatoes. They have a wonderful crispy crust and are delightfully easy to prepare.

Serves 6–8

200g/7oz Agen prunes

15g/$\frac{1}{2}$oz/1 tbsp butter

1 Spanish (Bermuda) onion, chopped

15ml/1 tbsp chopped fresh parsley

500g/1$\frac{1}{4}$lb boned loin of pork, with rind on

salt and ground black pepper

For the hasselback potatoes

1.3–1.8kg/3–4lb small roasting potatoes

100g/4oz/$\frac{1}{2}$ cup butter, melted

30ml/2 tbsp fresh breadcrumbs

Cook's tip Hasselback potatoes, with their delicious crispy shells, are named after the "Hasselbacken" restaurant of Stockholm where they were first served. The cooking times are adapted here to fit with the recipe, but if you are cooking them on their own, just put them in an oven preheated at 220°C/425°F/Gas 7 for 35–40 minutes.

1 Soak the prunes in cold water overnight. The next day, chop the prunes into small pieces. Melt the butter in a frying pan, add the onion and fry for about 5 minutes until beginning to soften. Add the chopped prunes and parsley and fry, stirring occasionally, until the onions are very soft and the mixture is slightly sticky. Season the mixture with salt and pepper to taste. Leave to cool while preparing the hasselback potatoes.

2 Preheat the oven to 220°C/425°F/Gas 7. Peel the potatoes so that they are evenly sized and oval. Put the potatoes, one at a time, on a wooden spoon and slice across their width at 5mm/$\frac{1}{4}$in intervals, through the potato until you hit the wooden spoon. This stops you slicing all the way through. Then put the potatoes in a roasting pan and pour over the melted butter. Roast in the top of the oven for 10 minutes.

3 Meanwhile, open out the pork and place, skin side down, on a chopping board. Spread the prune stuffing over the pork, roll up and tie at regular intervals with string. Using a sharp knife score the skin then sprinkle with salt.

4 When the potatoes have roasted for 10 minutes, baste with the butter. Reduce the oven temperature to 180°C/350°F/Gas 4 and roast the pork in the oven, below the potatoes, for 40 minutes.

5 When the pork has roasted for 40 minutes, remove the potatoes from the oven, baste and sprinkle over the breadcrumbs. Return to the oven and roast the potatoes and pork for a further 20 minutes.

6 Remove the cooked pork from the oven and leave it to stand for 15 minutes. Meanwhile increase the oven temperature to 220°C/425°F/Gas 7 and roast the potatoes for a further 15 minutes until golden brown and opened up like a fan. To serve, remove the crackling from the pork and carve the meat. Accompany with the hasselback potatoes.

Per portion Energy 538kcal/2247kJ; Protein 16.7g; Carbohydrate 42.8g, of which sugars 15.1g; Fat 34.6g, of which saturates 18.5g; Cholesterol 95mg; Calcium 46mg; Fibre 4g; Sodium 248mg.

Serves 8

8 salted pig's cheek oysters

1 leek, halved widthways

1 carrot, halved widthways

1 bay leaf

bouquet garni (see Cook's tip)

2 large swedes (rutabagas), chopped

250ml/8fl oz/1 cup crème fraîche

25g/1oz/2 tbsp butter

salt and ground black pepper

Cook's tip Make a bouquet garni by tying together a sprig of thyme, some parsley stalks and a sprig of marjoram.

Braised pig's cheeks with mashed swedes
Brasserad griskind med kålrotmos

This dish is usually made with ham hock but this method instead uses pig's cheeks as the main ingredient. Pig's cheek is deliciously tender and is now a more regular sight in fashionable restaurants.

1 Put the pig's cheeks in a pan and cover with cold water. Add the leek, carrot, bay leaf and bouquet garni, bring to the boil then lower the heat and simmer for 2 hours until tender.

2 Half an hour before the pig's cheeks are cooked, cook the swedes in boiling salted water for 30 minutes until soft. Drain, return to the pan and mash well. Add the crème fraîche and butter, season generously with pepper then mash again. Finally beat gently to make the mixture fluffy.

3 When the pig's cheeks are cooked, slice and serve hot with the mashed swedes.

Per portion Energy 272kcal/1131kJ; Protein 18.1g; Carbohydrate 8.6g, of which sugars 8.2g; Fat 18.6g, of which saturates 11.2g; Cholesterol 89mg; Calcium 99mg; Fibre 3.2g; Sodium 101mg.

Christmas ham with Swedish mustard
Julskinka med senap

At Christmas time in Sweden every possible use is made of almost all parts of the pig. This dish is always made with "green", or salted gammon, rather than the smoked variety. On Christmas Eve it is traditional to eat ham such as this for supper after having eaten a Christmas porridge, which is similar in style to rice pudding.

1 Put the gammon joint in a large pan. Add the onion, apples, bay leaves, peppercorns, thyme, parsley and cumin seeds and add enough water to cover. Bring to the boil then reduce the heat and simmer gently for 1 hour. Remove from the heat and leave to cool overnight in the pan.

2 Preheat the oven to 220°C/425°F/Gas 7. Remove the ham from the pan (don't discard the stock but see Cook's tip) and remove the rind from the ham, leaving the fat. Spread the mustard over the fat and sprinkle the breadcrumbs on top.

3 Put the ham in a roasting pan and bake in the oven for about 20 minutes until golden brown and crisp on the outside. Serve the ham hot or cold, with boiled peas and Cumberland sauce.

Per portion Energy 214kcal/893kJ; Protein 23.9g; Carbohydrate 4.9g, of which sugars 1g; Fat 11.7g, of which saturates 3.2g; Cholesterol 29mg; Calcium 32mg; Fibre 0.2g; Sodium 1313mg.

Serves 6–8

1kg/2¼lb unsmoked gammon (ham) joint

1 onion, halved

2 apples, quartered

2 bay leaves

5ml/1 tsp whole white peppercorns

2 sprigs fresh thyme

2–3 sprigs fresh parsley

5ml/1 tsp cumin seeds

2 tbsp Swedish mustard

30ml/2 tbsp fresh breadcrumbs

Boiled peas and Cumberland sauce, or other fruit sauce, to serve

Cook's tip Make good use of the stock from this recipe in a soup, known as Dopp-i-grytta. Bring the stock to the boil for about a minute and serve with a Swedish sweet bread, such as Vörtbröd.

Baked sausage terrine with lingonberry conserve
Korv terrine med lingon

This dish can be made with ready-made sausage meat (bulk sausage), or if you prefer you can make your own, as shown here, using a mixture of oatmeal, pig's liver, pork and raisins. The oatmeal gives a texture just like the sausage meat. The sweet lingonberry conserve is a perfect accompaniment.

Serves 6–8

115g/4oz/1 cup oatmeal

750ml/1¼ pints/3 cups water

750ml/1¼ pints/3 cups milk

15g/½oz/1 tbsp butter

1 red onion, finely chopped

200g/7oz pig's liver, minced (ground)

200g/7oz minced (ground) pork

150g/5oz/1 cup raisins

5ml/1 tsp chopped fresh marjoram

5ml/1 tsp ground allspice

salt and ground black pepper

lingonberry conserve and toast, to serve

1 Preheat the oven to 180°C/350°F/Gas 4. Line the base and sides of a 20cm/8in loaf tin (pan) with greaseproof (waxed) paper.

2 Put the oatmeal, water and milk in a large pan, bring to the boil then reduce the heat and cook for 3–4 minutes until soft. Leave to cool.

3 Melt the butter in a pan, add the finely chopped onion and fry for 5–10 minutes until the onion is softened. Transfer the onion to a large bowl, add the cooled oatmeal, pig's liver, minced pork, raisins, marjoram, allspice, salt and pepper and mix well together.

4 Pour the mixture into the prepared tin, level the top and bake in the oven for 40 minutes–1 hour until lightly browned. Serve the sausage terrine, hot or cold, with lingonberry conserve and toast.

Per portion Energy 238kcal/1003kJ; Protein 15.6g; Carbohydrate 28.5g, of which sugars 17.8g; Fat 7.7g, of which saturates 3.1g; Cholesterol 91mg; Calcium 134mg; Fibre 1.5g; Sodium 105mg.

Serves 6–8

50g/2oz/¹⁄₂ cup plain (all-purpose) flour

6–8 thin slices calf's liver, about 500g/1¹⁄₄lb

6–8 rashers (strips) streaky (fatty) bacon

15g/¹⁄₂oz/1 tbsp butter

30ml/2 tbsp capers

salt and ground black pepper

mashed potatoes, to serve

For the garnish

vegetable oil, for deep-frying

a bunch fresh parsley

Cook's tip As a variation, lamb's liver can be used in place of calf's liver.

Calf's liver with bacon and capers
Kalv lever med bacon och kapris

Liver and bacon is a classic pairing in Sweden, as elsewhere, and for good reason – they're a great combination. The addition of pickled capers, with their strong, slightly bitter flavour, adds piquancy and beautifully complements the delicately flavoured liver.

1 To prepare the garnish, heat the oil in a large pan or deep-fryer to 180ºC/350ºF or until a cube of bread, dropped into the fat, turns brown in 1 minute. Fry the parsley until crisp, then remove from the pan with a slotted spoon and drain on kitchen paper.

2 Spread the flour on a large plate and season with salt and pepper. Dip the liver slices in the flour and coat on both sides.

3 Put the bacon in a frying pan and fry in its own fat until crisp. Remove from the pan to a warmed dish and set aside. The bacon can be left whole or, if preferred, cut into small pieces.

4 Melt the butter with the bacon fat in the frying pan. Add the liver slices and fry for about 2 minutes on each side until cooked on the outside but still pink in the centre. Transfer the liver to a warmed serving dish.

5 Add the capers to the pan and fry for 1–2 minutes. Pour the capers over the liver, add the bacon and sprinkle with the fried parsley to garnish. Serve hot, with mashed potatoes.

Per portion Energy 178kcal/742kJ; Protein 16.5g; Carbohydrate 4.9g, of which sugars 0.1g; Fat 10.4g, of which saturates 3.9g; Cholesterol 254mg; Calcium 15mg; Fibre 0.2g; Sodium 410mg.

Sweetbreads with pancetta
Kalvbräss med rökt skinka

Lamb's sweetbreads tend to be more frequently used than other types of pancreas, but this recipe uses calf's sweetbreads. These have a mild taste but the addition of pancetta, salted belly of pork from Italy, adds a delicious contrasting flavour to the dish.

1 Soak the sweetbreads in cold water overnight. The next day, drain and put the sweetbreads in a pan. Cover with cold water, add 5ml/1 tsp salt and bring to the boil. Lower the heat and simmer for 5 minutes. Drain and leave to cool. When cool enough to handle, peel off any outer membrane and remove any veins. Cut the sweetbreads into small pieces.

2 Melt the butter in a frying pan. Add the sweetbreads and fry for 2–3 minutes to sear them. Using a slotted spoon, remove from the pan and set aside. Stir the flour into the pan then slowly add the cream, stirring all the time, to form a smooth sauce. Stir in the sherry and bring to the boil, stirring until the sauce thickens, then reduce the heat and simmer for about 5 minutes.

3 Meanwhile, cut the pancetta into thin strips. Put in a frying pan and fry in its own fat until crisp. Add the sweetbreads to the sauce and season with salt and cayenne pepper to taste. Serve the sweetbreads on toast with the crisp pancetta and sprinkle chopped parsley on top to garnish.

Per portion Energy 309kcal/1280kJ; Protein 14.1g; Carbohydrate 2g, of which sugars 0.5g; Fat 26.8g, of which saturates 13.9g; Cholesterol 220mg; Calcium 22mg; Fibre 0.1g; Sodium 387mg.

Serves 6–8

500g/1¼lb fresh or frozen calf's sweetbreads

25g/1oz/2 tbsp butter

15ml/1 tbsp plain (all-purpose) flour

200ml/7fl oz/scant 1 cup double (heavy) cream

30ml/2 tbsp dry Amontillado sherry

200g/7oz thinly sliced pancetta

salt and cayenne pepper

toast, to serve

chopped fresh parsley, to garnish

Wild
meat

Stuffed guinea fowl with
    wild mushrooms

Reindeer stroganoff

Roe deer cutlets with
    mushrooms

Elk meatballs with lingon

Carpaccio of cured venison

Elk kalops

Braised hare stew with
    juniper berries

Reindeer, guinea fowl
juniper berries and lingon

Sweden is noted for the quality of its wild meat. Reindeer, in particular, is a regional favourite. These animals are farmed in the north of Sweden but represent free-range organic meat at its best because they run freely and have few restrictions. Reindeer meat is dark red, very lean and tender and is also available smoked. Suitable replacements for reindeer meat are roe deer, any other venison or beef.

Elk (moose) is another popular wild meat in Sweden. Elk meat has many health-giving properties as it is high in vitamin A and iron and very low in fat. Elk wander unhindered in the woods during the summer and are only hunted between November and January. Beef is a convincing substitute in any recipe if elk meat is unavailable.

In Lappland, a province in northernmost Sweden, the local population regularly eats brown bear, but it is not readily available in other parts of Sweden so it doesn't feature in the following selection of recipes. In fact, the bear is a dangerous predator and reindeer farmers have to watch their herds carefully, especially after the bears emerge hungry from hibernation.

Wild hare (jackrabbit) and fowl are also eaten, including goose and eider duck, the latter being common in the Baltic regions. Duck meat tends to have a hint of fish because of the duck's staple diet, but this only adds to the flavour.

Serves 8

25g/1oz/2 tbsp butter, plus 15g/½oz/ 1 tbsp for the gravy

250g/9oz mixed wild mushrooms, chopped

30ml/2 tbsp chopped fresh parsley

5ml/1 tsp soy sauce

8 guinea fowl breast portions, skinned

about 750ml/1¼ pints/3 cups chicken stock for poaching

1 tbsp plain (all-purpose) flour

salt and ground black pepper

For the pearl barley risotto

200g/7oz pearl barley (see Cook's tips)

15ml/1 tbsp olive oil

100g/4oz mixed wild mushrooms

2 garlic cloves, crushed

100g/4oz fresh parsley, chopped

For the roasted vegetables

200g/7oz parsnips and carrots, or seasonal vegetables

120ml/4fl oz/½ cup olive oil

Cook's tips
• There are two ways to prepare pearl barley: either soak it in cold water for at least 4 hours before cooking for an hour; or cook it straight from the packet for approximately 2 hours.
• Pearl barley risotto can also be eaten as a dish on its own, sprinkled with grated Parmesan cheese and drizzled with truffle oil.

Stuffed guinea fowl with wild mushrooms
Pärlhöna med blandad svamp

Guinea fowl meat is white like chicken but tastes more like pheasant, although with a less gamey flavour. Here, the meat is combined with the earthy taste of wild mushrooms and served with pearl barley risotto.

1 Cook the pearl barley in a pan of lightly salted water for 1–2 hours until tender. Melt 25g/1oz/2 tbsp of the butter in a pan, add the mushrooms and sauté until the juices have evaporated. Add the parsley and soy sauce and leave to cool.

2 Put the guinea fowl portions between 2 sheets of clear film (plastic wrap) and bash until flattened with a wooden rolling pin. Spread the cold mushroom stuffing on to the guinea fowl portions then roll them up carefully. Wrap each individually in clear film.

3 Preheat the oven to 180°C/350°F/Gas 4. Cut the vegetables into strips or cubes and put in an oiled roasting pan. Drizzle with the olive oil, sprinkle with salt and roast in the oven for approximately 20 minutes until tender.

4 Thirty minutes before the barley is cooked, put the wrapped breasts in a pan in a single layer and pour over the stock. Bring to the boil and simmer gently for 30 minutes.

5 Ten minutes before the barley is cooked, prepare the pearl barley risotto. Heat the oil in a pan, add the mushrooms and sauté. Remove the cooked breasts from the stock and keep warm. Pour the stock into a jug (pitcher) and make up to 600ml/1 pint/2½ cup if required.

6 Melt the remaining butter, add the flour, and cook, stirring over a low heat for 1 minute to make a roux. Remove from the heat and add the reserved stock to form a gravy. Return to the heat and stir for 2–3 minutes until the gravy thickens. Season to taste.

7 Drain the pearl barley and add to the mushrooms with the garlic and parsley. Stir together. Unwrap the breasts, slice carefully and place on warmed serving plates. Serve with the gravy, roasted vegetables and pearl barley risotto.

Per portion Energy 348kcal/1462kJ; Protein 27.7g; Carbohydrate 26g, of which sugars 2.4g; Fat 15.6g, of which saturates 3.6g; Cholesterol 77mg; Calcium 49mg; Fibre 1.8g; Sodium 226mg.

Serves 6–8

1kg/2¼lb reindeer, roe deer or beef fillet

15g/½oz/1 tbsp butter

15ml/1 tbsp vegetable oil

2 Spanish (Bermuda) onions, chopped

8 juniper berries, crushed

15ml/1 tbsp plain (all-purpose) flour

45ml/3 tbsp tomato purée (paste)

45ml/3 tbsp Dijon mustard

475ml/16fl oz/2 cups double (heavy) cream

chopped fresh parsley, to garnish

boiled rice or pearl barley, to serve

Cook's tip Garnishing the stroganoff with chopped parsley gives the dish more colour and freshness.

Reindeer stroganoff
Ren stroganoff

The fillet used in this dish is the best cut of reindeer. The bitter gin flavour of the juniper berries is a strong complement to the wild meat. Beef is an excellent substitute meat or, for a more authentic taste, use roe deer which is similar to reindeer in texture and taste.

1 Cut the meat into 5mm/¼in x 5cm/2in strips. Heat the butter and oil in a large flameproof casserole, add the meat and fry for about 5 minutes until golden brown on all sides. Add the onions and juniper berries.

2 Stir the flour into the pan then, over a low heat, add the tomato purée, mustard and finally the cream and stir together. Simmer for about half an hour until the meat is tender. Garnish the dish with chopped parsley and serve with boiled rice or pearl barley.

Per portion Energy 486kcal/2019kJ; Protein 30.2g; Carbohydrate 7.8g, of which sugars 5.1g; Fat 38.2g, of which saturates 22g; Cholesterol 148mg; Calcium 57mg; Fibre 0.9g; Sodium 274mg.

Roe deer cutlets with mushrooms
Rådjur med svamp

Wild roe deer, a species of Europe and Asia Minor, is very popular in Sweden and its flesh has the lowest fat content of any red meat. Roe deer is a good substitute for reindeer and is very tender. Blackberries, redcurrants and juniper berries are all classic flavours to add to roe deer or other venison dishes – this recipe uses juniper berries.

1 In a large frying pan, melt 25g/1oz/2 tbsp of the butter, add all the mushrooms and sauté until browned. Meanwhile, season the cutlets with salt and pepper. Melt 25g/1oz/2 tbsp of the butter in a flameproof casserole, add the cutlets and fry for 2–3 minutes until browned on both sides.

2 Add the water, shallots, juniper berries, thyme and bay leaf to the cutlets. Bring to the boil then simmer for 10 minutes to reduce the liquid.

3 Meanwhile, melt half the remaining butter in a large frying pan. Add the potatoes and fry for about 20 minutes, stirring occasionally, until golden brown. Transfer to a serving dish and keep warm. Fry the carrots in the remaining butter until golden.

4 Add the cream to the casserole and continue to cook for 20 minutes. Finally, add the sautéed mushrooms. Serve hot, with the fried potatoes and carrots.

Per portion Energy 455kcal/1903kJ; Protein 40.7g; Carbohydrate 19.3g, of which sugars 6.8g; Fat 25.4g, of which saturates 14.7g; Cholesterol 137mg; Calcium 50mg; Fibre 3g; Sodium 193mg.

Serves 6

75g/3oz/6 tbsp butter

200g/7oz chanterelle (girolle) mushrooms, halved if large

200g/7oz trumpet mushrooms (trompette des morts)

2kg/4½lb saddle of roe deer (12 cutlets), trimmed by the butcher

1 litre/1¾ pints/4 cups water

3 shallots, chopped

5 juniper berries, crushed

1 fresh thyme sprig, chopped

1 bay leaf

225g/8oz potatoes, cut into 5mm/¼in cubes

6 small carrots, cut into 5mm/¼in cubes

120ml/4fl oz/½ cup double (heavy) cream

salt and ground black pepper

Elk meatballs with lingon
Alg Köttbullar med lingon

Meatballs are probably the best-known Swedish dish and are especially delicious when home-made. When making them yourself, always make a large quantity to make the most of your time because they do take a while to prepare. This method suggests using half the meatballs and freezing the rest.

1 Cut the potato into quarters and cook in boiling water for 15–20 minutes until tender, then drain and mash. Melt 75g/3oz/16 tbsp of the butter in a frying pan, add the onions and fry until softened.

2 Put the mashed potato, onions, breadcrumbs, cream and milk in a large bowl and mix together. Leave to swell for a few minutes then add the sugar, season generously with pepper and add the salt. Add the elk or pork and steak mince, the eggs and parsley and mix thoroughly together. Leave to stand for 1 hour to allow the flavours to infuse.

3 Roll the mixture into meatballs that are about the size of a small apricot. (At this stage, if it is more convenient you can freeze half the quantity of meatballs to use on another occasion.)

4 Heat the remaining butter and the oil in a large frying pan, add the meatballs and fry in batches to avoid over-crowding the pan, for about 10 minutes until browned. (You may need to add a little more oil to the pan but this will depend on how much fat there is in the meat.) Using a slotted spoon, remove the meatballs from the pan, transfer to a warmed serving dish and keep warm.

5 To make the cream sauce, add the sherry to the pan and stir to deglaze the pan. Stir in the cream, add the soy sauce if using, and heat gently. Pour the sauce over the meatballs and serve hot, with mashed potatoes and lingonberry conserve.

Per portion Energy 1655kcal/6860kJ; Protein 79.6g; Carbohydrate 40.7g, of which sugars 13.2g; Fat 129.2g, of which saturates 64.8g; Cholesterol 552mg; Calcium 205mg; Fibre 3.2g; Sodium 666mg.

The meatballs serve 12–14; the sauce serves 6

1 large potato

100g/4oz/$\frac{1}{2}$ cup butter

1kg/2$\frac{1}{4}$lb red onions, finely chopped

150g/5oz/2$\frac{1}{2}$ cups fresh breadcrumbs

300ml/$\frac{1}{2}$ pint/1$\frac{1}{4}$ cups double (heavy) cream

105ml/7 tbsp full-fat (whole) milk

5ml/1 tsp sugar

ground white pepper

10ml/2 tsp salt

3kg/6$\frac{3}{4}$lb minced (ground) elk (moose) or 1kg/2$\frac{1}{4}$lb best quality minced (ground) pork and 2kg/4$\frac{1}{2}$lb best quality minced (ground) steak

6 eggs, beaten

handful of finely chopped fresh parsley

about 45ml/3 tbsp vegetable oil

mashed potatoes and lingonberry conserve, to serve

For the cream sauce

120ml/4fl oz/$\frac{1}{2}$ cup Amontillado sherry

250ml/8fl oz/1 cup double (heavy) cream

30ml/2 tbsp soy sauce (optional)

Cook's tip

To make good quality minced (ground) pork, buy a boneless leg of pork and for minced steak, buy topside or braising steak. Having trimmed off the fat, mince (grind) the meat in a food processor or mincer.

1kg/2¼lb venison fillet

50g/2oz/½ cup sea salt

50g/2oz/¼ cup caster (superfine) sugar

1 bunch fresh thyme, leaves stripped

5ml/1 tsp ground black pepper

olive oil and lemon juice, for drizzling

crisp green salad and Melba toast, to serve

Carpaccio of cured venison
Tunt skivat gravad hjort

Carpaccio of venison is a modern cured-meat dish. It is a good alternative to gravlax and is prepared in a similar way, the only difference being that fresh thyme flavours the meat instead of dill. You can use elk, reindeer or any other venison for this dish. Because it needs to be prepared in advance and frozen, the dish requires a little preparation on the day.

1 Remove all stringy parts from the venison fillet then place on a sheet of foil. Mix the salt and sugar together and sprinkle the mixture over the fillet. Add the thyme leaves and season with pepper.

2 Wrap the fillet in the foil and leave in the refrigerator to cure for 48 hours, turning every 12 hours. Transfer the fillet to the freezer and store for up to 1 week before serving.

3 Thinly slice the meat while it is still frozen, when it is much easier to slice. Thaw the fillet for a minimum of 10 hours in the refrigerator. Just before serving, place the sliced meat on serving plates and drizzle with a little olive oil and lemon juice. Serve with a crisp green salad and Melba toast.

Per portion Energy 153kcal/651kJ; Protein 27.8g; Carbohydrate 6.5g, of which sugars 6.5g; Fat 2.8g, of which saturates 1g; Cholesterol 63mg; Calcium 10mg; Fibre 0g; Sodium 69mg.

Elk kalops
Älg kalops

Kalops is the Swedish word for meat pieces or stew, and this recipe uses elk thigh, which is the best cut of all. Although it is not necessary to use this cut when making kalops, it does reduce cooking time. A good tip is to include a small piece of bone (with marrow), which gives the sauce an extra richness.

1 Cut the meat into 1cm/½in cubes. Heat the butter and oil in a flameproof casserole. Add the meat and fry for about 5 minutes until browned on all sides. Using a slotted spoon, remove from the pan and set aside.

2 Add the onions to the pan and fry for about 10 minutes, stirring occasionally, until softened. Add the carrots and fry for a further 2–3 minutes then add the bay leaves, allspice, pepper and salt. Stir in the flour then return the meat to the pan. Slowly stir in the wine and beef stock, bring to the boil then cover and simmer for about 2 hours until very tender. Serve with pickled beetroot.

Per portion Energy 136kcal/571kJ; Protein 14.6g; Carbohydrate 5.5g, of which sugars 3.1g; Fat 4.4g, of which saturates 1.7g; Cholesterol 35mg; Calcium 21mg; Fibre 0.9g; Sodium 52mg.

Serves 6–8

1kg/2¼lb elk (moose) thigh

15g/½oz/1 tbsp butter

15ml/1 tbsp vegetable oil

2 Spanish (Bermuda) onions, roughly chopped

2 carrots, roughly chopped

3 bay leaves

5ml/1 tsp ground allspice

5ml/1 tsp ground white pepper

15ml/1 tbsp plain (all-purpose) flour

250ml/8fl oz/1 cup red wine

500ml/17fl oz/2¼ cups beef stock

salt

pickled beetroot (beet), to serve

Cook's tip Pickled beetroot (beet), is a classic Swedish accompaniment to meat. It can be bought ready prepared or made fresh, and can be stored in the refrigerator for up to three weeks.

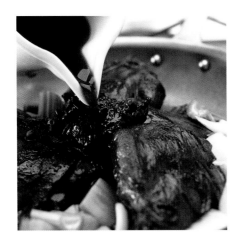

Braised hare stew with juniper berries
Har stuvning med enbär

Hare is very popular in Sweden, where it is readily available, and cooking it in a stew gives it a wonderful wild taste without being too strong. A young hare needs less time for braising than an older one so check its age as well as asking the butcher to cut it into joints for you. You can make your own pickled cucumbers following the recipe below, or buy them ready made.

1 If making pickled cucumbers, prepare them several days in advance. Put the cucumber slices in a large bowl, sprinkling them with the salt. Add the water, cover and leave for 2 days.

2 Preheat the oven to 140°C/275°F/Gas 1. Thoroughly wash and rinse several preserving jars. Place on a baking tray and dry in the oven while cooking the cucumbers.

3 Drain and rinse the cucumber slices under cold running water. Put the vinegar, sugar and pickling spice in a preserving pan and put over a medium heat. Bring to the boil, stirring until the sugar has dissolved. Add the cucumber slices and boil for 2–3 seconds.

3 Pack the cucumber slices into the prepared hot jars and fill with the hot vinegar liquid. Cover immediately with airtight, vinegar-proof tops. Store the jars in a cool, dark place until required.

4 To make the hare stew, melt 15g/½oz/1 tbsp of the butter with the vegetable oil in a large, heavy pan. Add the hare joints and fry for about 15 minutes until browned on all sides.

5 Add the onion, carrot, celery, red wine, blackcurrant jelly, juniper berries, thyme, bay leaf, salt and pepper. Bring to the boil then simmer until the wine has almost evaporated. Add the water, cover and simmer for a further 35 minutes until the meat is tender, adding more water if necessary to prevent it from becoming dry. Transfer the meat to a warmed serving dish, cover with foil and keep warm.

6 Strain the stock through a sieve (strainer) into a clean pan. Put the remaining butter in a small bowl and beat until soft. Add the flour and blend together to form a smooth paste. Heat the stock in the pan and add small pieces of the butter mixture, whisking or stirring vigorously until each piece has melted before adding another piece. Bring to the boil then simmer, stirring all the time, until the sauce becomes creamy. Stir in the cream. Pour the sauce over the meat, garnish with parsley sprigs and serve with rowanberry jelly and pickled cucumbers.

Serves 6–8

25g/1oz/2 tbsp butter

15ml/1 tbsp vegetable oil

1 oven-ready hare (jackrabbit), cut into 9–10 pieces

1 onion, roughly chopped

1 carrot, roughly chopped

2 celery sticks, roughly chopped

200ml/7fl oz/scant 1 cup red wine

15ml/1 tbsp blackcurrant jelly

8 juniper berries, crushed

1 fresh thyme sprig and 1 bay leaf

475ml/16fl oz/2 cups water

15ml/1 tbsp plain (all-purpose) flour

200ml/7fl oz/scant 1 cup double (heavy) cream

salt and ground black pepper

parsley sprigs, to garnish

rowanberry jelly and pickled cucumbers (see below), to serve

For the pickled cucumbers (optional)

1.6kg/3½lb medium cucumbers, sliced

185g/6½oz salt

3.8 litres/6½ pints/16¼ cups water

1.2 litres/2 pints/5 cups white vinegar

1kg/2¼lb/5 cups sugar

15ml/1 tbsp whole pickling spice

Per portion Energy 336kcal/1400kJ; Protein 25.5g; Carbohydrate 4.7g, of which sugars 3g; Fat 22.3g, of which saturates 12.4g; Cholesterol 101mg; Calcium 50mg; Fibre 0.5g; Sodium 109mg.

Desserts

Rosehip soup

Glögg jelly with clove cream

Swedish apple cake with
vanilla cream

Almond stuffed baked apples

Almond pears

Wild berry tart

Waffles with spiced blueberry
compote

Cloudberry soufflé

Saffron pancake

Rosehips, cloudberries,
cloves and vanilla cream

Swedes of all ages love eating sweet foods, and no meal
would be seen as complete without a dessert, whether hot or
cold, simple, or rich and indulgent.

This chapter collects together a tantalizing selection of
Swedish desserts. Almonds are a popular ingredient and
feature again and again in these recipes in such favourites
as Almond Stuffed Baked Apples, Almond Pears and
Swedish Apple Cake. Sweden is blessed with an exquisite
variety of wild and cultivated berries, such as lingonberries,
cloudberries and blueberries as well as strawberries and
blackberries, and these are also a key ingredient in many
delicious desserts, such as Wild Berry Tart, Waffles with
Spiced Blueberry Compote and Cloudberry Soufflé.

The saffron in the pancake that appears here gives it an
unusual spicy taste, and this recipe, for an extra kick, includes
a shot of vodka. Rosehip Soup is another unusual and quite
delightful treat, again using wild berries. Rosehips are
seasonal and can be collected and used from your own
garden, but some specialist flower shops are able to get
supplies all year round.

Serves 4–6

600–700g/1lb 6oz–1lb 9oz fresh or
400–500g/14oz–1¼lb dried rosehips

2 litres/3½ pints/8 cups water

15ml/1 tbsp cornflour (cornstarch)

100g/4oz/½ cup sugar

whipped double (heavy) cream or vanilla
ice cream, to serve

Rosehip soup
Nyponsoppa

In Scandinavia fruit soups are often eaten as a dessert – rosehip is the most popular, and blueberry is another favourite. Those who like this richly coloured red soup can pick wild rosehips every autumn – it is highly nutritious and a welcome sweet treat in the winter months.

1 If using fresh rosehips, cut in half then scoop out every trace of the seeds and prickly hairs. If using dried rosehips, put in a mortar and grind with a pestle.

2 Put the rosehips in a pan, add the water, bring to the boil and simmer for about 30 minutes until they are soft. Bring to the boil and boil for 15 minutes to reduce the liquid.

3 Strain the rosehips through muslin (cheesecloth) and reserve the liquid. In a small bowl, blend the cornflour with a little of the liquid to form a smooth paste. Pour the reserved liquid into a pan and add the sugar. Slowly stir in the cornflour mixture and slowly bring to the boil, stirring all the time, then simmer for 10–15 minutes until slightly thickened. Pour into cups or bowls and serve warm or cold with a spoonful of whipped cream or ice cream on top.

Per portion Energy 92kcal/391kJ; Protein 0.8g; Carbohydrate 22.8g, of which sugars 20.5g; Fat 0.3g, of which saturates 0.1g; Cholesterol 0mg; Calcium 16mg; Fibre 1g; Sodium 11mg.

Cook's tip The soup is also good served with a spoonful of freshly ground blanched almonds instead of the whipped cream or ice cream.

Glögg jelly with clove cream
Glögg med nejlika grädde

This delicious sweet was the result of a happy accident – some Glögg wine left over after a party and the inspired idea to make jelly with it.

1 Soak the gelatine leaves in cold water until soft. Pour the Glögg wine into a pan and heat gently.

2 Stir the sugar into the wine until dissolved then add the softened gelatine leaves, which should melt in the hot wine. Pour the mixture into individual heatproof serving glasses, leave to cool, then place in the refrigerator for about an hour to set.

3 Whisk the cream until stiff then add the icing sugar and ground cloves. Just before serving, add a spoonful of the cream to each glass of jelly.

Per portion Energy 1577kcal/6524kJ; Protein 4g; Carbohydrate 24.8g, of which sugars 24.8g; Fat 107.4g, of which saturates 66.8g; Cholesterol 274mg; Calcium 161mg; Fibre 0g; Sodium 98mg.

Serves 6–8

5 gelatine leaves

750ml/1¼ pints Swedish Glögg or mulled wine

15ml/1 tbsp sugar

For the spiced cream

200ml/7fl oz/scant 1 cup double (heavy) cream

5ml/1 tsp icing (confectioner's) sugar

pinch of ground cloves

Cook's tip Swedish Glögg is a mulled wine that is usually enjoyed at Christmas. It is served hot and has a robust alcohol content.

Swedish apple cake with vanilla cream
Appelkaka med vaniljkräm

Swedish apples are very sweet and ideally suited to this sublime cake. Apples form a significant part of Sweden's produce and survive the cold winters well. Kivik, a harbour town in Skåne in southern Sweden, is well known for its apple market and holds an annual festival where a huge picture is created, made entirely of apples.

1 Preheat the oven to 180°C/350°F/Gas 4. Butter a 20cm/8in flan tin (pan) using 15g/½oz/1 tbsp of the butter. Peel, core and thinly slice the apples and put the slices in a bowl. Add the caster sugar and cinnamon and mix them together. Put the mixture in the prepared tin.

2 Put the remaining butter and sugar in a bowl and whisk them together until they are light and fluffy. Beat in the egg yolks, then add the almonds and lemon rind and juice to the mixture.

3 Whisk the egg whites until stiff then fold into the mixture. Pour the mixture over the apples in the flan tin. Bake in the oven for about 40 minutes until golden brown and the apples are tender.

4 Meanwhile, make the vanilla cream. Put the milk, cream, sugar and vanilla pod in a pan and heat gently. Add a little of the warm milk mixture to the eggs then slowly add the egg mixture to the pan and continue to heat gently, stirring all the time, until the mixture thickens. Do not allow the mixture to boil or it will curdle.

5 Remove the vanilla pod and serve the vanilla cream warm or cold with the apple cake.

Serves 6–8

115g/4½oz/½ cup plus 1 tbsp unsalted (sweet) butter

7 eating apples

30ml/2 tbsp caster (superfine) sugar

10ml/2 tsp ground cinnamon

200g/7oz/1 cup sugar

2 egg yolks and 3 egg whites

100g/4oz/1 cup ground almonds

grated rind and juice of ½ lemon

For the vanilla cream

250ml/8fl oz/1 cup milk

250ml/8fl oz/1 cup double (heavy) cream

15ml/1 tbsp sugar

1 vanilla pod (bean), split

4 egg yolks, beaten

Serving variations
• Serve the apple cake with 300ml/½ pint/1¼ cups double (heavy) cream to which you have added 5ml/1 tsp vanilla sugar.
• Alternatively, serve with vanilla ice cream, which is particularly good if the cake is served warm.

Per portion Energy 541kcal/2254kJ; Protein 7.6g; Carbohydrate 39.7g, of which sugars 39.3g; Fat 40.3g, of which saturates 20g; Cholesterol 227mg; Calcium 122mg; Fibre 2.1g; Sodium 135mg.

Almond stuffed baked apples

Drottningäpplen

The first spoonful of this baked apple dessert is always a delightful surprise. The pastry wrapping the apple acts as an enclosed oven which bakes the apple and keeps in its flavour, and this mingles perfectly with the almonds.

1 To make the pastry, put the flour in a food processor. Cut the butter into small pieces, add to the flour and then, using a pulsating action, mix together until the mixture resembles fine breadcrumbs. Add the sugar and egg and mix to form a dough. Wrap in greaseproof (waxed) paper and place in the refrigerator for 1 hour.

2 Preheat the oven to 200°C/400°F/Gas 6. To make the almond stuffing, melt the butter and leave to cool but not set. Put the ground almonds, caster sugar and cinnamon in a bowl. Add the melted butter and mix together. Remove the cores from the apples and then use the stuffing to fill their centres.

3 Divide the pastry into 8. On a floured surface, roll each piece about 5mm/¼in thick and, using a plate, cut into a 20–23cm/8–9in round. Put a round over the top of each apple and wrap the pastry around, pinching it in at the bottom. Place on a baking tray.

4 Beat the egg yolk and water together and brush over the pastry to glaze. Bake in the oven for about 30 minutes until golden brown. Serve hot, with the vanilla-flavoured cream.

Per portion Energy 735kcal/3080kJ; Protein 11.2g; Carbohydrate 87.7g, of which sugars 32.6g; Fat 40.2g, of which saturates 20.6g; Cholesterol 129mg; Calcium 159mg; Fibre 5.2g; Sodium 245mg.

Serves 8

8 eating apples

1 egg yolk

30ml/2 tbsp water

double (heavy) cream, whipped with 5ml/1 tsp vanilla sugar, to serve

For the pastry

575g/1¼lb/5 cups plain (all-purpose) flour

225g/8oz/1 cup unsalted (sweet) butter

100g/4oz/½ cup caster (superfine) sugar

1 egg, beaten

For the almond stuffing

25g/1oz/2 tbsp unsalted (sweet) butter

100g/4oz/1 cup ground almonds

50g/2oz/4 tbsp caster (superfine) sugar

10ml/2 tsp ground cinnamon

Serves 8

8 large ripe pears

juice of 1 lemon

25g/1oz/2 tbsp unsalted (sweet) butter

350g/12oz/2 cups ground almonds

475ml/16fl oz/2 cups double
(heavy) cream

Almond pears
Mandelpäron

This old-fashioned Swedish baked dessert is a tempting combination of cooked fruit and a sprinkling of ground almonds. The cream melts with the juices and ground almonds to form a delicious sauce.

1 Preheat the oven to 180°C/350°F/Gas 4. Peel and halve the pears and remove the cores. Put the pears into an ovenproof dish and sprinkle with lemon juice to stop them going brown.

2 Put a small piece of butter on each pear and sprinkle the ground almonds evenly over the top. Bake in the oven for about 15 minutes, basting once or twice with the juice, until they begin to soften.

3 Meanwhile, whisk the cream until it is beginning to hold its shape. When the pears are cooked, pour over the whipped cream and serve immediately.

Per portion Energy 607kcal/2511kJ; Protein 10.5g; Carbohydrate 15.3g, of which sugars 14.1g; Fat 56.4g, of which saturates 21.8g; Cholesterol 81mg; Calcium 147mg; Fibre 5.7g; Sodium 23mg.

Serves 6–8

500g/1¼lb fresh or frozen mixed wild berries

200g/7oz/1 cup caster (superfine) sugar

whipped double (heavy) cream, to serve

For the pastry

300g/10oz/2½ cups plain (all-purpose) flour

115g/4oz/½ cup unsalted (sweet) butter

50g/2oz/¼ cup caster (superfine) sugar

1 egg, beaten

Cook's tip Instead of cooking the fruit in the tart, you can make the tart and then fill it with uncooked fresh berries. Bake the pastry case for a further 10 minutes, leave it to cool and then brush the base with melted plain (semisweet) chocolate. Leave to set and then fill with fresh berries. The chocolate will stop the berries from softening the pastry before the tart is served.

Wild berry tart
Skogsbär flan

The Swedish forests abound in wild berries, including lingonberries, cloudberries, bilberries and strawberries. The cool climate and evening sunshine create their magical taste, which improves the further north you go. When cooking, Swedes will often reject perfect uniform shapes in favour of small, irregular berries whose flavour they regard as superior. If wild berries are out of season, this tart is equally delicious made with cultivated berries that are available all year round.

1 To make the pastry, put the flour in a food processor. Cut the butter into small pieces, add to the flour and then, using a pulsating action, mix together until the mixture resembles fine breadcrumbs.

2 Stir in the sugar and add the egg to the mixture and combine to form a dough. Wrap in greaseproof (waxed) paper and place in the refrigerator for 1 hour.

3 Preheat the oven to 180°C/350°F/Gas 4. On a lightly floured surface, roll out the pastry thinly and use to line a 20cm/8in flan tin (pan).

4 Put a circle of greaseproof paper in the pastry case (pie shell) and fill with baking beans. Bake in the oven for 10–15 minutes until the pastry has set. Remove the paper and beans and return to the oven for 5 minutes until the base is dry.

5 Fill the tart with the berries and sugar. Then return the tart to the oven and bake for a further 5–10 minutes until the pastry is golden brown. Serve warm with whipped cream.

Per portion Energy 618kcal/2601kJ; Protein 8g; Carbohydrate 98.1g, of which sugars 43.3g; Fat 24.2g, of which saturates 14.9g; Cholesterol 60mg; Calcium 141mg; Fibre 3.8g; Sodium 177mg.

Waffles with spiced blueberry compote
Våflor med blåbärs kompott

This recipe requires a waffle iron. If you have to purchase one it is unlikely that you will ever regret it, since waffles are so popular and are equally delicious with other stewed fruits or maple syrup. The blueberry compote can also be served with grilled goat's cheese, pancakes or rice pudding.

1 To make the spiced blueberry compote, put the blueberries into a pan, then add the sugar, vinegar, cinnamon and cloves and poach for about 5 minutes until soft and liquid. Bring to the boil and cook for a further 4 minutes to reduce the liquid. Either keep the compote warm, or cool and store in the refrigerator for up to 1 month.

2 To make the waffles, melt the butter. Put the flour in a large bowl and gradually beat in the water to form a smooth mixture then add the melted butter. Whisk the cream until stiff then fold into the mixture.

3 Preheat a waffle iron according to the manufacturer's instructions. Add a little butter to grease the waffle iron then place a dollop of waffle mixture in the iron. Cook the waffles until golden and crispy, keep warm and continue to cook the remaining waffle mixture, greasing the iron each time with a little butter. Serve hot with the spiced blueberry compote.

Per waffle Energy 189kcal/787kJ; Protein 2.12g; Carbohydrate 14.52g, of which sugars 1.18g; Fat 14.03g, of which saturates 8.62g; Cholesterol 35mg; Calcium 41mg; Fibre 0,85g; Sodium 14mg.

Makes 20

25g/1oz/1 tbsp unsalted (sweet) butter, plus extra for greasing

350g/12oz/3 cups plain (all-purpose) flour

350ml/12fl oz/1½ cups water

475ml/16fl oz/2 cups double (heavy) cream

For the spiced blueberry compote

200g/7oz blueberries, fresh or frozen

15ml/1 tbsp sugar

5ml/1 tsp balsamic vinegar

pinch of ground cinnamon

pinch of ground cloves

Variation Instead of the blueberry compote, serve the waffles with whipping cream and lingon conserve.

Serves 6–8

50g/2oz/4 tbsp unsalted (sweet) butter, plus extra for greasing

60ml/4 tbsp plain (all-purpose) flour

475ml/16fl oz/2 cups milk

4 egg yolks and 6 egg whites

275g/10oz/1 cup cloudberry jam

30ml/2 tbsp Lakka (Finnish cloudberry liqueur)

Cloudberry soufflé
Hjortron sufflé

With cloudberries as the main ingredient, this dish is undeniably Scandinavian. Cloudberries are rare little golden raspberry-like berries with an exquisite taste that only grow wild in northern Scandinavia. Fresh ones are rarely available elsewhere, but the jam can be found in specialist stores.

1 Preheat the oven to 180°C/350°F/Gas 4. Grease an 18cm/7in soufflé dish with butter. Melt the butter in a pan, add the flour and cook over a low heat for 30 seconds, stirring to make a roux. Slowly add the milk, stirring continuously, to form a smooth sauce. Cook until the sauce boils and thickens.

2 Remove the sauce from the heat, leave to cool slightly then stir in the egg yolks. Add the cloudberry jam and cloudberry liqueur and turn into a large bowl.

3 In a large, separate bowl, whisk the egg whites until stiff then, using a metal spoon, fold them into the sauce. Put the mixture into the prepared soufflé dish and bake in the oven for about 20 minutes until risen. Serve the soufflé immediately.

Per portion Energy 284kcal/1198kJ; Protein 6.7g; Carbohydrate 44.9g, of which sugars 37.4g; Fat 9g, of which saturates 4.7g; Cholesterol 118mg; Calcium 102mg; Fibre 0.2g; Sodium 129mg.

Cook's tips
• The cloudberry jam could be replaced with another fruit jam.
• The cloudberry liqueur could be replaced with brandy or another fruit liqueur, such as crème de mûre or crème de framboise.

Saffron pancake
Saffran pankakor

This dessert originates from Gotland, an island off the south-east coast of Sweden. It is traditionally served with salmberry (a local berry) jam and whipped cream. The dish is superstitiously associated with the number seven – it is said that in its preparation seven ingredients should come from Gotland, seven spices should come from hot countries and seven pieces of wood should be used in the fire for the oven. It is served at Christmas, weddings and other festive occasions.

1 If you want to make almond paste to replace the mazipan, put the almonds in a food processor and, using a pulsating action, chop until finely ground. Add the sugar and egg white and mix to form a paste. The prepared almond paste can then be stored in a plastic bag in the refrigerator for up to 3 days until required.

2 Grease a 20cm/8in flan tin (pan) with butter. Then put the rice and water in a pan and cook as directed on the packet or until the rice is tender and the water has been absorbed.

3 Once the water has been absorbed, add the milk and salt and continue to cook, stirring occasionally so that it does not stick, for a further 30 minutes. Meanwhile, put the vodka in a small bowl, add the saffron and leave to soak.

4 Preheat the oven to 220°C/425°F/Gas 7. Add the honey to the cooked rice mixture then grate in the marzipan or almond paste. Stir gently then add the saffron vodka, cardamom and cinnamon. Finally, add the beaten eggs and flour and mix together.

5 Turn the mixture into the prepared flan tin and bake in the oven for about 30 minutes until golden brown. Scatter with the toasted flaked almonds and serve warm, with jam and whipped cream.

Per portion Energy 5957kcal/4015kJ; Protein 24.8g; Carbohydrate 141g, of which sugars 85.8g; Fat 34g, of which saturates 4.5g; Cholesterol 195mg; Calcium 273mg; Fibre 3.6g; Sodium 131mg.

Serves 6–8

400g/14oz/2 cups short grain rice

475ml/16fl oz/2 cups water

475ml/16fl oz/2 cups milk

5ml/1 tsp salt

30ml/2 tbsp vodka

pinch of saffron threads

225g/8oz/1 cup clear honey

150g/5oz good quality marzipan or almond paste (see below)

5ml/1 tsp ground cardamom

2.5ml/½ tsp ground cinnamon

6 eggs, beaten

5ml/1 tsp plain (all-purpose) flour

50g/2oz/½ cup toasted flaked (sliced) almonds, to decorate

jam and whipped cream, to serve

For the almond paste (optional)

200g/7oz/1½ cups blanched almonds

200g/7oz/1¾ cups icing (confectioners') sugar

1 egg white

Cook's tip Any leftover almond paste can be made into chocolate marzipan balls to serve with coffee, by adding a little unsweetened cocoa powder to the mixture and rolling it into balls.

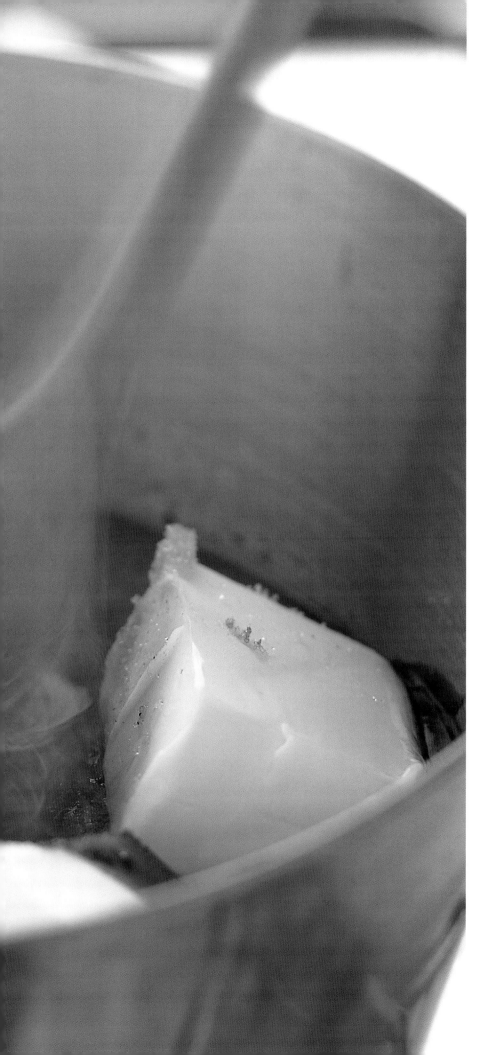

Baking

Crumbly, creamy
and gooey

Baking and bakeries form an integral part of Swedish life. Indeed, Stockholm has more bakeries than any other type of food store. Swedes love to drink coffee, which is invariably accompanied by a bun, cake or biscuit. This routine is called "fika", which means to take a break and have a coffee and a sweet snack with your colleagues, friends or family. It is an ingrained social institution in Sweden.

Almonds often appear in traditional Swedish baking, featuring especially at Christmas and Easter. They are used in the glamorous bright-green Princess Cake that is found in every Swedish bakery as well as the gluten-free Chocolate Gooey Cake (Choklad Kladd Kaka).

Spices also feature frequently in Swedish baking. Gingerbread Biscuits, or Pepparkakor, are Sweden's best-known biscuits and these are flavoured with ginger, cinnamon, cloves and cardamom. Saffron, another popular spice, is the key ingredient in Lucia Saffron Buns.

The selection of recipes introduced here also includes two for savoury breads, Tunnbröd and Knäckebröd, although these are only a fraction of the many available.

Makes 20

300ml/½ pint/1¼ cups milk

130g/4½oz/9 tbsp unsalted (sweet) butter

a pinch of saffron threads

50g/2oz fresh yeast

700g/1½lb/6 cups plain (all-purpose) flour

5ml/1 tsp salt

150g/5oz/¾ cup caster (superfine) sugar

40 raisins

beaten egg, to glaze

Cook's tip These buns are traditionally made in any number of shapes. They include the shape of a cat, an S shape, a braided wreath, a figure of eight or a crown, the latter representing the crown of St Lucia.

Lucia saffron buns
Lussekatter

On the 13th December, the Swedes celebrate the Italian festival of Saint Lucia to combat the effects of a long dark winter. These festival buns, flavoured with saffron, are made early in the morning of that day. They are called lussekatter, or "Lucia cats", because this is one of the shapes that are used for the buns.

1 Put the milk and butter in a pan and heat until the butter has melted. Remove from the heat, add the saffron threads and leave to cool until warm to the touch.

2 In a large bowl, blend the fresh yeast with a little of the warm saffron milk. Add the remaining saffron milk then add the flour, salt and sugar. Mix together to form a dough that comes away from the sides of the bowl.

3 Turn the dough on to a lightly floured surface and knead for about 10 minutes until the dough feels firm and elastic. Shape into a ball, put in a clean bowl and cover with a clean dish towel. Leave to rise in a warm place for about 1 hour until the dough has doubled in size.

4 Turn the dough on to a lightly floured surface and knead again for 2–3 minutes. Divide the dough into 20 equal pieces. Form each piece into a roll, and then shape each roll into an S shape and place on greased baking sheets.

5 Place a raisin at the end of each bun. Cover with a clean dish towel and leave to rise in a warm place for about 40 minutes until doubled in size.

6 Preheat the oven to 200°C/400°F/Gas 6. Brush the tops of the buns with beaten egg to glaze and bake in the oven for about 15 minutes until golden brown.

Per bun Energy 423kcal/1788kJ; Protein 9.2g; Carbohydrate 81.7g, of which sugars 15.1g; Fat 8.8g, of which saturates 5g; Cholesterol 20mg; Calcium 161mg; Fibre 2.8g; Sodium 69mg.

Fat Tuesday buns
Semlor

Fat Tuesday Buns, or Shrove Tuesday Buns, are only eaten in the months of January and February in Sweden, up until the beginning of Lent. They are so meltingly delicious it always seems a pity to restrict their availability until then. The recipe can incorporate ready-made marzipan, but an even better idea is to make your own using the almond paste recipe shown below.

1 If you want to make almond paste to replace the marzipan, put the almonds in a food processor and, using a pulsating action, chop until finely ground. Add the sugar and egg white and mix to form a paste. The prepared almond paste can then be stored in a plastic bag in the refrigerator for up to 3 days until required.

2 Pour the cream into a pan and heat gently until warm to the touch. In a separate pan, gently melt the butter.

3 In a large bowl, blend the yeast with a little of the warmed cream and then add the melted butter, cardamom and sugar. Add the flour and salt and mix together to form a dough.

4 Turn the dough on to a lightly floured surface and knead for about 10 minutes until the dough feels firm and elastic. Shape into a ball, put in a clean bowl and cover with a clean dish towel. Leave to rise in a warm place for about 1½ hours until the dough has doubled in size.

5 Turn the dough on to a lightly floured surface and knead again for 2–3 minutes. Divide the dough into 12 equal pieces. Shape each piece into a round bun and place on a greased baking sheet. Cover with a clean dish towel and leave to rise in a warm place until doubled in size.

6 Preheat the oven to 180°C/350°F/Gas 4. Brush the tops of the buns with beaten egg to glaze then bake in the oven for about 10 minutes until golden brown. Transfer to a wire rack and leave to cool.

7 To serve, cut the tops off the buns and reserve. Remove about half of the dough from the buns and put in a bowl. Grate the marzipan or almond paste into the bowl and mix together. Replace the mixture in the buns.

8 Whisk the cream until stiff, top the buns with the whipped cream and then replace the tops. Sprinkle the icing sugar on top of each bun and either serve on individual serving plates or in a deep bowl with warmed milk, the traditional way of serving them in Sweden.

Makes 12

275ml/16fl oz/2 cups double (heavy) cream

100g/4oz/½ cup unsalted (sweet) butter

40g/1½oz fresh yeast

5ml/1 tsp ground cardamom

30ml/2 tbsp sugar

450g/1lb/4 cups plain (all-purpose) flour

pinch of salt

1 egg, beaten

icing (confectioners') sugar, to decorate

warmed milk, to serve (optional)

For the filling

100g/4oz good quality marzipan or almond paste (see below)

275ml/16fl oz/2 cups double (heavy) cream

For the almond paste (optional)

100g/4oz/¾ cup blanched almonds

100g/4oz/½ cup icing (confectioners') sugar

½ an egg white

Cook's tip When making the almond paste, you can buy blanched almonds or you can blanch them yourself by popping them into boiling water and then sliding off their skins.

Per bun Energy 465kcal/1938kJ; Protein 5.3g; Carbohydrate 38.2g, of which sugars 9.6g; Fat 33.4g, of which saturates 19.9g; Cholesterol 96mg; Calcium 85mg; Fibre 1.3g; Sodium 69mg.

Ginger biscuits
Pepparkakor

These biscuits are found all over Sweden. There is even a Swedish nursery rhyme saying that if you are good you will be given Pepparkakor but if you are bad you will be given none! You can cut the biscuits into any shape, but stars and hearts are the traditional forms.

1 Put the butter, sugar, syrup, treacle, ginger, cinnamon, cloves and cardamom in a heavy pan and heat gently until the butter has melted.

2 Put the bicarbonate of soda and water in a large heatproof bowl. Pour in the warm spice mixture and mix well together then add the flour and stir until well blended. Put in the refrigerator overnight to rest.

3 Preheat the oven to 220°C/425°F/Gas 7. Line several baking sheets with baking parchment. Knead the dough then roll out on a lightly floured surface as thinly as possible. Cut the dough into shapes of your choice and place on the baking sheets.

4 Bake the biscuits in the oven for about 5 minutes until golden brown, cooking in batches until all the biscuits are cooked. Leave to cool on the baking sheet.

Per portion Energy 31kcal/130kJ; Protein 0.2g; Carbohydrate 5.8g, of which sugars 4.2g; Fat 0.8g, of which saturates 0.5g; Cholesterol 2mg; Calcium 5mg; Fibre 0.1g; Sodium13mg.

Makes about 50

150g/5½oz/½ cup plus 3 tbsp butter

400g/14oz/2 cups sugar

50ml/2fl oz/¼ cup golden (light corn) syrup

15ml/1 tbsp treacle (molasses)

15ml/1 tbsp ground ginger

30ml/2 tbsp ground cinnamon

15ml/1 tbsp ground cloves

5ml/1 tsp ground cardamom

5ml/1 tsp bicarbonate of soda (baking soda)

240ml/8fl oz/1 cup water

150g/5oz/1¼ cups plain (all-purpose) flour

15g/½oz/1 tbsp unsalted (sweet) butter

350g/12oz/3 cups plain (all-purpose) flour

5ml/1 tsp baking powder

120ml/4fl oz/½ cup double (heavy) cream

5 egg yolks, beaten

vegetable oil, for deep-frying

200g/7oz/1 cup caster (superfine) sugar

Swedish deep-fried cakes
Klenäter

These small, deep-fried cakes, which are similar to doughnuts, are an essential part of the Christmas celebrations in Sweden. The characteristic Klenäter form is created by cutting a hole in every pastry strip and threading one end through the hole in the middle, making a sort of knot in the middle of the pastry.

1 Melt the butter and then leave to cool but not set. Sift the flour and baking powder into a large bowl. Add the cream, egg yolks and melted butter and beat together with a wooden spoon to form a smooth dough. Leave the dough to rest for about 2 hours.

2 On a lightly floured surface, thinly roll out the dough into a rectangle. Cut into 1cm/½in strips, and then cut each strip into 5cm/2in pieces. Cut a slit in the centre of each piece, fold each piece in half and then put one end through the hole and press down to flatten the cake.

3 Heat the oil in a large pan or deep-fryer to 180°C/350°F or until a cube of bread, dropped into it, turns brown in 1 minute. Put the sugar on a large plate.

4 Drop the cakes, in batches so that the pan is not overcrowded, into the hot oil and cook, turning once with a slotted spoon, until they are golden brown and crispy. Remove and drain on kitchen paper. Transfer the cakes to the sugar and turn them to dust them in the sugar. Serve them warm or cold.

Per portion Energy 436kcal/1830kJ; Protein 6.3g; Carbohydrate 60.4g, of which sugars 27.1g; Fat 20.5g, of which saturates 7.9g; Cholesterol 151mg; Calcium 97mg; Fibre 1.4g; Sodium 23mg.

Coconut cakes
Kokostopar

These popular, moist coconut cakes, similar to coconut macaroons, are commonplace in Sweden. They are best served straight from the oven, but also keep reasonably well in the freezer or in an airtight container.

1 Split open the vanilla pod and put in a pan with the cream. Heat gently until bubbles start to form round the edge of the pan then remove from the heat and leave to infuse for 20 minutes.

2 Preheat the oven to 200°C/400°F/Gas 6. Line a baking sheet with greaseproof (waxed) paper. Remove the vanilla pod from the cream and pour the cream into a bowl. Add the coconut, sugar and egg and mix together.

3 Spoon the mixture in piles on to the prepared baking sheet. Bake in the oven for 12–15 minutes until golden brown and a little crisp on top. Leave the cakes to cool slightly before transferring to a cooling rack.

Per cake Energy 177kcal/740kJ; Protein 1.4g; Carbohydrate 14.9g, of which sugars 14.9g; Fat 13g, of which saturates 9.9g; Cholesterol 23.6mg; Calcium 16mg; Fibre 1.8g; Sodium 10.9mg.

Makes 15–20

1 vanilla pod (bean)

120ml/4fl oz/½ cup double (heavy) cream

200g/7oz desiccated (dry unsweetened shredded) coconut

200g/4oz/1 cup caster (superfine) sugar

1 egg

Cook's tip Don't discard the vanilla pod after you have used it to make the vanilla cream. Rinse it well, leave to dry and then keep it in a jar to use another time. Alternatively, put it in a jar of sugar to make vanilla sugar.

Serves 8

100g/4oz dark (bittersweet) chocolate with 75 per cent cocoa solids

5ml/1 tsp water

100g/4oz/½ cup unsalted (sweet) butter, plus extra to grease

2 eggs, separated

175g/6oz/1½ cups ground almonds

5ml/1 tsp vanilla sugar

whipped double (heavy) cream, to serve

Chocolate gooey cake
Choklad kladd kaka

This is Sweden's favourite chocolate cake. For perfect results it is essential to undercook the cake so that it is dense in the middle. Made with almonds instead of flour, Choklad Kladd Kaka is gluten free and therefore the perfect tempting, self-indulgent snack for a coeliac guest.

1 Preheat the oven to 180°C/350°F/Gas 4. Grease a 20cm/8in shallow round cake tin (pan) with butter. Break the chocolate into a pan. Add the water and heat gently until the chocolate has melted. Remove from the heat.

2 Cut the butter into small pieces, add to the chocolate and stir until melted. Add the egg yolks, ground almonds and vanilla sugar and stir together. Turn the mixture into a large bowl.

3 Whisk the egg whites until stiff then fold them into the chocolate mixture. Put the mixture into the prepared tin and bake in the oven for 15–17 minutes until just set. The mixture should still be soft in the centre. Leave to cool in the tin. When cold, serve with whipped cream.

Per portion Energy 311kcal/1288kJ; Protein 6.8g; Carbohydrate 10g, of which sugars 9.3g; Fat 27.4g, of which saturates 9.9g; Cholesterol 75mg; Calcium 66.2mg; Fibre 1.9g; Sodium 97mg.

Princess cake
Princesstårta or

A Swedish cookbook would not be complete without a recipe for that self-indulgent classic, the Princess Cake. With its distinctive light-green marzipan coating, it swells with whipped cream, sponge cake and jam. Traditionally, a pink rose crowns the top, but here fresh strawberries are used.

Serves 8–10

200g/7oz/scant 1 cup unsalted (sweet) butter, plus extra for greasing

400g/14oz/2 cups caster (superfine) sugar

3 eggs

350g/12oz/3 cups plain (all-purpose) flour

5ml/1 tsp baking powder

10ml/2 tsp vanilla sugar

a few drops of green food colouring

250g/9oz good quality marzipan or almond paste (see below)

icing (confectioners') sugar, to dust

fresh strawberries, to serve

For the filling and topping

3 gelatine leaves

1 litre/1¾ pints/4 cups double (heavy) cream

10ml/2 tsp sugar

10ml/2 tsp cornflour (cornstarch)

2 egg yolks

10ml/2 tsp vanilla sugar

For the almond paste (optional)

200g/7oz/1½ cups blanched almonds

200g/7oz/1¾ cups icing (confectioners') sugar

1 egg white

1 If you want to make almond paste to replace the marzipan, put the almonds in a food processor and, using a pulsating action, chop until finely ground. Add the sugar and egg white and mix to form a paste. The prepared almond paste can then be stored in a plastic bag in the refrigerator for up to 3 days until required.

2 Preheat the oven to 180°C/350°F/Gas 4. Grease a 20cm/8in round cake tin (pan) with butter. Put the butter and sugar in a large bowl and whisk together until fluffy. Add the eggs and whisk together. Sift in the flour and baking powder, add the vanilla sugar and stir together.

3 Turn the mixture into the prepared cake tin and bake in the oven for 1 hour until golden brown and firm to the touch. Remove the cake from the oven and leave to cool in the tin. When the cake is cold, slice in half horizontally.

4 To make the filling, soak the gelatine leaves in cold water until soft or according to the directions on the packet. Put 500ml/17fl oz/2 cups of the cream, the sugar, cornflour and egg yolks in a pan and heat gently, stirring all the time, until the mixture thickens. Do not allow the mixture to boil or the eggs will curdle. Pour the mixture into a bowl, add the soaked gelatine leaves and leave to cool but not set.

5 Put the remaining cream in a bowl, add the vanilla sugar and whisk until stiff. Fold the whisked cream into the cooled custard and before it thickens spread half the custard over the bottom layer of cake. Put the other cake layer on top and spread over the remaining custard.

6 Add a few drops of green food colouring to the marzipan or almond paste and knead until evenly coloured. Between 2 sheets of foil or greaseproof (waxed) paper, thinly roll out the marzipan or almond paste into a round. Remove the top sheet of foil or greaseproof paper and, using a large plate at least 30cm/12in in diameter, cut the marzipan into a circle.

7 Using the foil or greaseproof paper to lift the marzipan, carefully place the marzipan circle over the top of the cake and tuck it down the sides of the cake to make it look like a green dome. Sprinkle a little icing sugar on top and serve with fresh strawberries.

Per portion Energy 1326kcal/5512kJ; Protein 11.3g; Carbohydrate 112.1g, of which sugars 77.6g; Fat 95.7g, of which saturates 56.1g; Cholesterol 346.4mg; Calcium 191.5mg; Fibre 1.9g; Sodium 218.7mg.

Makes 8–12

500g/1lb 2oz/4½ cups plain (all-purpose) flour

5ml/1 tsp salt

200ml/7fl oz/scant 1 cup milk

Cook's tip These bread pancakes will retain their taste when served a day later.

Thin breads made in a pan
Tunnbröd

This thin pancake is similar to tortilla bread and originates from Lappland in the north of Sweden, where it was traditionally baked in an open fireplace. It is popular to serve tunnbröd with sausages and mashed potatoes.

1 Put a large heavy frying pan over a medium heat. Put the flour and salt in a bowl then gradually add the milk and mix together to form a dough.

2 Turn the dough out on to a lightly floured surface and knead for about 2 minutes. Cut the dough into 8–12 equal pieces then roll each piece into a thin, flat round.

3 Put a round in the hot pan and fry for about 2 minutes, then turn over and cook the second side for a further 2 minutes. Transfer to a large plate and cook the remaining rounds in the same way, stacking one on top of another. Leave to cool on a plate.

Per portion Energy 150kcal/637kJ; Protein 4.5g; Carbohydrate 33.2g, of which sugars 1.4g; Fat 0.8g, of which saturates 0.3g; Cholesterol 1mg; Calcium 78mg; Fibre 1.3g; Sodium 8mg.

Home-made crisp rye breads
Knäckebröd

These traditional crispbreads were originally made with a hole in the centre so they could be hung over the oven to keep dry. Nowadays, they keep well in an airtight container. Knäckebröd is also sometimes made with rolled oats, in a similar way to sweet Scottish oatcakes.

1 Put the milk in a pan and heat gently until warm to the touch. Remove from the heat. In a bowl, blend the yeast with a little of the warmed milk. Add the remaining milk then add the rye flour, bread flour, caraway or cumin seeds and salt and mix together to form a dough.

2 Using the rye flour for dusting, turn the dough out on to a lightly floured surface and knead the dough for about 2 minutes. Cut the dough into 15 equal pieces then roll out each piece into a thin, flat round. Place on baking sheets and leave to rise in a warm place for 20 minutes.

3 Preheat the oven to 150°C/300°F/Gas 2. Using the rye flour, roll out the pieces of dough again into very thin, flat rounds. Return to the baking sheets. Make a pattern on the surface using a fork or knife.

4 Bake the breads in the oven for 8–10 minutes, turning after about 5 minutes, until hard and crispy. Transfer to a wire rack and leave to cool. Store the breads in an airtight container.

Per portion Energy 323kcal/1376kJ; Protein 9.2g; Carbohydrate 71.1g, of which sugars 2.4g; Fat 2.2g, of which saturates 0.7g; Cholesterol 2mg; Calcium 118mg; Fibre 7.3g; Sodium 19mg.

Makes 15

600ml/1 pint/2½ cups milk

50g/2oz fresh yeast

565g/1¼lb/5 cups rye flour plus 225g/8oz/2 cups, for dusting

565g/1¼lb/5 cups strong white bread flour

10ml/2 tsp caraway or cumin seeds

5ml/1 tsp salt

Cook's tip The Swedes use a special rolling pin with a knobbly surface to create the distinctive texture of this hard bread. An ordinary rolling pin is a good substitute, with the speckled texture created with the head of a fork or a knife end.

Suppliers

IKEA

The international Swedish chain IKEA has sites in Europe, North America, the Middle East and Asia Pacific. Each store has a Swedish food market stocking specialist ingredients – from Swedish meatballs to unrefined hard bread and caviar spread. Check your local IKEA store by visiting www.ikea.com

Internet suppliers

www.deli-shop.com
www.igourmet.com
www.swedensbest.com
www.swestuff.se

Australia

www.igourmet.com/australianfood
See also other internet suppliers listed above.

Sweden

H & W Linnevaror
(kitchen utensils and table linens)
Övre Husargatan 15/204
SE-413 14 Gothenburg
Tel: 011-46-31/133729
martin@how.se; www.how.se

ICA ute i världen
(food specialities such as caviar, sill, surströmming and chocolate)
niklas.gloggler@nara.ica.se
www.icasvensktmat.se

The Northerner
(gifts, food and crafts)
Flöjelbergsgatan 16A
43135 Mölndal, Sweden
Tel: 007 812 272 57 37
www.northerner.com

Swestuff Internetbutik
(internet food market)
info@swestuff.se
www.swestuff.se

United Kingdom

Upper Glas Restaurant
The Mall, 359 Upper Street
Islington, London N1 OPD
Tel: 020 7359 1932
www.glasrestaurant.co.uk

Scandelicious
Visit: Scandelicious at Borough Market
Southwark Street
London SE1 9AB

Contact: Scandelicious
4 Beaconsfield Road
Aldeburgh
Suffolk IP15 5HF
Tel: 01728 452880
www.scandelicious.co.uk

Totally Swedish
32 Crawford Street
London W1H 1LS
Tel: 020 7224 9300
info@totallyswedish.com
shop@totallyswedish.com

United States

American-Swedish Institute
Bookstore and Museum Shop
2600 Park Avenue
Minneapolis, MN 55407
Tel: 1-(800) 579-3336
www.americanswedishinst.org

Anderson Butik
PO Box 151
120 West Lincoln
Lindsborg, KS 67456
Tel: 001 (800) 782 4132
imports@andersonbutik.com
www.andersonbutik.com

Berolina Bakery Pastry Shop
(Cakes, pastries and fresh bread)
3421 Ocean View Blvd
Glendale, CA 91208
Tel: 001 (818) 249 6506

The Crown Bakery
133 Gold Star Blvd
Worcester, MA
Tel: 001 (508) 852-0746
www.thecrownbakery.com

Distinctively Sweden
15 Messenger Street
Plainville, MA 02762
Tel: 001 (508) 643-2676
www.distinctivelysweden.com

Genuine Scandinavia, LLC.
(kitchenware, crockery and accessories)
958 Washington Street, #9
Denver, CO 80203
Tel: 001 (303) 318 0714
Sales@GenuineScandinavia.com
www.GenuineScandinavia.com

The Gift Chalet
(Specializing in everything from Scandinavia, including food)
8 Washington Street – Route 20
Auburn, MA 01501
Tel: 001 (508) 755-3028
GiftChalet@aol.com
www.giftchaletauburn.com

Nordic Fox
(restaurant featuring Scandinavian foods)
10924 Paramount Blvd
Downey, CA 90241
Tel: 001 (562) 869 1414

Nordic House
3421 Telegraph Avenue
Oakland, CA 94609
Tel: 001 (510) 653-3882
pia@nordichouse.com
www.nordichouse.com

Olson's Delicatessen
(Scandinavian foods and gifts)
5660 West Pico Blvd
Los Angeles, CA
Tel: 001 (323) 938 0742

Scandia Food & Gifts Inc.
30 High Street
Norwalk, CT 06851
Tel: 001 (203) 838 2087
scandia@webquill.com
www.scandiafood.com

Scandinavian Marketplace
PO Box 274, 218 Second Street East, Hastings, MN 55033
Tel: 1-(800) 797-4319
steve@scandinavianmarket.com
www.scandinavianmarket.com

Signal Seafoods, Inc.
(Swedish crayfish delivered to all of North America)
7355 SW 240th Place
Beaverton, OR
Tel: 001 (503) 626 6342
sales@crayfishparty.com
www.crayfishparty.com

Simply Scandinavian Foods
99 Exchange Street
Portland, ME 04101
Tel: 001 (207) 874 6759; 001 (877) 874 6759 (toll free)
info@simplyscandinavian.com
www.simplyscandinavian.com

Wikström's Gourmet Food
5247 North Clark Street
Chicago, IL 60640
Tel: 001 (773) 275 6100
sales@wikstromsgourmet.com
www.wikstromsgourmet.com

Index

Publisher's acknowledgements

Thank you to Lucy McKelvie for
the home economy, William
Lingwood for the photography ,
Helen Trent for the styling and
Simon Daley for the design.

The publishers would like to
thank the following for permission
to reproduce their images: p6
Mary Evans Picture Library; p7r
blickwinkel/Alamy; p8t Frank
Chmura/Alamy; p8b Chad Ehlers
Alamy; p9 Chad Ehlers/Alamy;
p10t Chad Ehlers/Alamy; p10b
Jason Lindsey/Alamy; p13br JHB
Photography/Alamy; p14l Chad
Ehlers/Alamy; p14r Chad
Ehlers/Alamy; p15b Robert
Harding Picture Library. t=top,
b=bottom, r=right
All other photographs © Anness
Publishing Ltd.

Author's acknowledgements

Many thanks to my darling
husband John who has tasted
and tested all my recipes; and
to Johan Berggren who taught
me all the difficult and
interesting things about
Swedish cooking; to Fanny
Kulmala my parents' cook; and
last but not least my aunt Beata,
my guru and educator (see
below), and after whom I named
one of my daughters.